WHAT ARE WE THINKING? IT MATTERS.

Dana Lichtstrahl

LIGHTBEAM
B O O K S

ISBN: 0977784444
ISBN-13: 978-0977784448

1. Consciousness. 2. Body, mind & spirit. 3. Healing. 4. Non-
Fiction. 5. Psychology. 6. Social sciences. 7. Wellness.

DEDICATED to those who wonder . . .

*"Why can't we then will positive states
of mind into existence?"*

— The Book of Soulspeak

CONTENTS

You seek knowledge from books, ridiculous!
You seek pleasure from sweets, ridiculous!
You are the sea of knowledge hidden in a dewdrop;
you are the universe hidden in a body three yards long.

— Rumi

The only important thing in a book
is the meaning that it has for you.
— W. Somerset Maugham

NOTE TO READER

The reason I began researching, writing and wanting to fully understand the process of thinking, was the suicide of a good friend, of my youngest son, in 2014.

What triggered such a thought — to jump; then the action to follow?

I became submerged in the question; Do we think up everything we think . . . about, or does thinking JUST happen?

Fear is the cheapest room in the house.
I would like to see you living in better conditions.
— Hafiz

INTRODUCTION

And in response to the question, "What makes this book different?," we can say with certainty that it delivers a new identity paradigm, (Identity defined as: who we think we are; who we understand ourselves to be).

We come to find out that thinking is, more accurately, our entire body-mind-spirit system at work, processing, all that we encounter. And all that processing happens 24/7, whether we're aware of it, or not.

We also come to understand that *becoming aware of,* (observing, watching, knowing . . .) *all that thinking happening,* (ideas, beliefs, dreams, etc. — all that we can become aware of), *establishes a rock-solid center-of-Self,* (Awareness as center-of-Self), *establishing a new identification — such that we become more compassionate with one another, and more at peace with ourselves.*

Is the system already caring for itself?

1. SNAP, CRACKLE, EXPLODE!

"*I had a kitchen knife in my hand,*" she said with a crazy smile, as she frantically ran up to me looking with intensity into my eyes, almost apologetic. I had just arrived home. I had never seen her like this. We stood just outside my front door. Her frenzy was still present. She continued, "*I thought I was going to push it through him,* '*I really did!*'" I began listening more intently. Was she aware of what she was saying?

We say people snap into violent or other realities, and don't "snap out of it." Some of us snap for an hour, or an instant into anger, or laughter and then return to a more balanced frame of mind, seeming to snap back into that. We can wonder what happened to control . . .

"*One day I'm just gonna snap and blow his f**king brains out!*"

He was fuming from the extreme dismissive and harsh behavior of a local police officer. I was too. Did we choose to think angry thoughts in an instant? Were we triggered, reflecting back the very violence we disliked? Someone else might not have flinched.

Something wasn't right about believing my thinking was "up to me." Was "I" truly in control of that? And if so, why wasn't I thinking more positive thoughts, most of the time?!

Which part of me wasn't thinking the way I wanted to and, why not?!

I read an article I haven't been able to find again, about how Mother Teresa, at a defining moment in her 20's, while walking across a fog-covered bridge one evening in Calcutta, encountered a man walking toward her. She couldn't see him clearly. If she was attacked, she imagined, she would kill him. Aware of that kind of thought and action, she instantly became, *intensely aware of her capacity for sudden rage and harm toward another,* and with all her power fled to the nearest church. And so her life as a compassionate, sympathetic savior unfolded. If that's true, why those thoughts, at that moment, and not another? And how did her awareness of that thought happen?

> *"I was in the woods." He quietly shared. "I came upon a tree that was hollow. I noticed there was just enough room for me to stand inside, so I did. Once there, almost instantly, I felt and saw that everything was an extension of myself, the tree, the woods, the sun; I was aware that I had never known such an overwhelming feeling of complete unity; it was all so remarkably extraordinary."*

Is that snapping too? Did it just happen? Was it planned? At that moment was he in control of his thoughts?

No matter which end of the expression-spectrum we experience (snap into?), it's clear we come equipped to think, feel and express intense fear, sadness, rage, joy, and even a kind of knowing; an awareness of all that thinking and experiencing.

As for timing, the possibility of snapping into every emotional experience exists. No research necessary. Empirical evidence proves our expressive-spectrum is our potential probabilities waiting to happen . . . with the right trigger? Or can we "control" ourselves, our thinking, our emotional-snapping — *especially if violent?*

On a dime I've snapped meanly at my kids, colleagues, parents, siblings, friends, dogs, etc. and I wondered why that tipping-point, why that thought and reaction, at that moment? Why do I, (we humans) do that in an instant? Do we craft that — in a flash?

Is war the snapping of global leadership?

The potential unpredictability of our own and another's behavior, scares the crap out of us and rightly so. We all know in a living-system — the human body to the entire Universe — things move and erupt, and eruption is unpredictable. It happens?! We have no say, (which can be enough to make anyone snap, depending on what you believe).

Thinking about it all kept happening. It was as if I was being taken for a ride . . . almost out of my control . . . I was aware there was more to understand . . .

"SURPRISE!" Walk into a surprise birthday party and in the blink of an eye, an assessment of, *"is this safe?,"* can pour through the entire body-mind-spirit system. Instantly the system is in a state of unplanned alert; the individual having had no agency (control) over their response. Pulse quickening, maybe sweats, thoughts of danger . . . and wham! Instant change. *"What the . . .!?"*

Ok, so, biologically during unpredictably fearful experiences, scientists have determined that in a tiny section they call the limbic system of the brain, sits the amygdala (one on each side), almost directly in the middle of the skull, in line behind the eyes, and it's always assessing danger, and then sparking a response to stimuli, accordingly. It ignites our adrenal glands, which sit just above the left and right kidney, to instantly secrete hormones and steroids that command our entire system into action if necessary, whatever action that may be, (not sticking the knife through?) That's phenomenal!

The system does its essential thing to stay steady and safe, managing its life. Have you heard of, *"fight, flight, freeze, or fawn response"* (we've actually labeled four ways our system reacts to something perceived as harmful — even thoughts)? Without us lifting a finger, stuff happens. Chaos is managed. Did you know that when rabbits, squirrels and other small animals encounter a snake, they can simply freeze. They become paralyzed and die. Is that their "chaos management"? Somehow they know they don't have a chance? Unpredictability inherent in all of it . . . ?

Is the system already caring for itself?

I hear from everywhere,
"It was out of my control!"
"It wasn't in my control!"
"I didn't like that I didn't have control!"
"Can you tell my greatest fear is loss of control?!"

Is the ultimate "lack of control" the unpredictable timing of our death; when the body stops functioning?

Can any of us say with seriousness, *"I have control in certain areas of my life, yet not in others"*? It seems much like believing, *"I think up some thoughts and not others."* Why is *that*? Why not *all* thoughts and all areas of my life?

I believe most of us were taught that we, *"had control over our life"* and so believed there was a "me" who did, and that became an aspect of our identity. "I'm in control." Is it true, accurate, helpful? And why did I keep running into, "having control," as a repeated important concern for most of us?! Did that have to do with what *we were taught*, about how we're in control of our thinking? And therefore our actions, behaviors, etc.? Was there a sense of freedom in having control?

In 2015 when I assisted my dad, Melvin A. Benarde, Ph.D., in publishing his book, *Germs Are Us: Collaborating FOR LIFE,* I noticed he had included a table showing "The Leading Causes of Death in the U.S. by Age Group." I was unpredictably shocked when I saw the ranking of causes. Wow. The most current stats he used were taken from the National Center for Health Statistics' (NCHS) 2011 report. (Such reports, lag behind the current year by a few years. In 2017, I read the new 2015 numbers and they hadn't changed much from 2011. I have yet to see newer ones.)

The 2nd leading cause of death for the 15-34 age group remained suicide. It was still the 3rd leading cause in the 10-14 age group, and the 4th for ages 35-44. It dropped off to 5th place after age 44 and after age 54, suicide moved into 8th place. As someone greatly interested in how thinking works, I became aware of the question; *"Is suicide death by thoughts?"* That was unpredictably unbearable . . .

I continued to wonder about the list. Homicide was in 3rd, 4th and 5th place from ages 1-44. Was homicide "death by thoughts" too; *"I'm gonna kill him!",* unless of course homicide was the 1st leading cause of death in that same age group, which was listed as "accidents"? Were accidents (which were considered "unintended"; all else were "intentional"), also "death by thoughts"? *"Why did she drive off the road — what was she thinking?!"*

Did thinking determine our life experience? Was it a kind of prison, or sanctuary?

Yes we snap, crackle and explode! And *w*hat if we aren't *"in control"* of any of our expressions — unpredictable, or otherwise? What if we don't choose all that thinking, those ideas, all that conceptual content, the way we understood; the way we were taught, the way we believe we function? What if we function very differently and . . . what if that really was truly great news?

I once heard Maya Angelou quote, Terence, a Playwright, and Poet who lived around 185 B.C. He had said, *"I am a human being. Nothing human is alien to me."* Somehow that was comforting.

I felt myself reconsidering beliefs about thinking I had been taught . . . The world was looking rounder.

What's in this book is,
1) the research that supports "thinking happens," (it's not something you do and I explain that),
2) why that's such fantastically great news, in relation to who we think we are, and,
3) how I became unexpectedly aware of our internal natural scales of justice — thinking and observing — that are built-in to us all; purposefully balancing all that thinking . . .

    and also . . .

4) how, if we're taught to observe all that thinking, all shackles dissolve, and I mean limitations. With the awareness of our thoughts, more possibilities show up. It's just what happens. We're hardwired for that. Almost immediate liberation happens with the big benefit *the certain reduction of stress* — every time. We move into a reality of extraordinary creative possibility and increased health. No high blood pressure, no nose bleeds, stomach aches, stiff necks . . . suicide?

This book offers what I discovered about thinking; which includes what every master has offered their disciples for

14

thousands of years; that *awareness is our essential, natural, built-in, system-balancing attribute, along with thinking.*

And with the practices throughout this book to strengthen those attributes, such knowledge is now out of the cave, the research lab and off the therapist's couch for easy use.

Chapters 2, 3 and 4 open the path to my quest for what and why I had to know. Prompt #1, the first practice to strengthen the ability to observe, follows chapter 4. Chapters 5 to 9 examine my burning question, and include a few more Prompts. Then in Chapters 10 through 13, we're on to further understanding, how beneficial change can be attained by practicing more Prompts toward establishing a shift; such that we become *more compassionate with one another, and more at peace with ourselves.*

Now about that burning question . . .

. . . it became clear that thinking is not a verb.

2. THE QUESTION

I had to know.

It seemed if I knew I would become authentically free, along with everyone else, from all that "monkey mind," which could be bushels of fearful, painful thoughts.

If I could share what I found — clearly — as I could hardly believe it myself; it would be a game-changer. What occurred along the way to finding out, included events like this . . .

> "You don't know the subject." He said very matter of fact. "That's why you're having trouble writing about it."

The subject had been a focus of mine for almost 5 years. I had just one burning question about how we humans work, or rather function. I had read the journals, the books, attended the lectures, events, watched the videos and movies *. . . how could he say I didn't know the subject?!* That hurt.

And why was I still so crazed over getting the answer to my question?! Would it finally release me from, *not understanding?* Would I then experience some kind of exceptional unlimited potential, or *authentic* freedom?!

I didn't recall asking to be interested in "the subject"; staying up late, reading other people's perspectives. Why did I care so much *and why did it suck me in!?* And why did my son's dear friend jump — to his death? Why hadn't other thoughts come for him? Why hadn't the words come to write about it? I felt mentally caged.

> So there we were, at the kitchen table having tea and I simply asked, *"What do you do when you're writing and the words don't come?"* I knew of at least 12 books he had written. His first response, *"You get up and go to the bathroom."* I smiled. Then out of his mouth rolled, *"You don't know the subject. That's why you're having trouble writing about it."*

> Instantly irritated I shot back with a puzzled look, *"Last September you read what I was writing and said it was wonderful! (. . . as I was thinking, WTF!)"*

It was now the following August and I was still knee deep in re-writing. I was wrestling with a subject that was new for everyone who was curious about it; *the process of thinking and its relationship to who, or what we humans think, we are.* To me, something seemed terribly inaccurate, wrong in fact, about how we understood thinking . . . which appeared to *determine our experiences* here; which included our sense of identity and peace.

Watching Shakespeare's, Henry V, Act 4, Scene 1, we hear, "There is some soul of goodness in evil, would men observingly distill it out." That felt spot on . . .

I knew the one and only burning question I wanted answered. It was sharp and clear . . .

> Q: *Do we (some sort of central "I," ego?), think up everything we think . . . about, or does thinking JUST happen?*

Get that? Does that make sense? I had to know. It mattered, because if thinking happens, and we're *not in control of it*, and we live believing that; if we're taught that, it would seriously reorient our relationship to all that's here: nature-made to man-made, *and certainly to ourselves*. If thinking happens it would turn our identity understanding upside down, significantly shifting our sense of life, which would offer an amazingly beneficial, *new life perspective;* as monumental as, *the world as we know it, no longer being flat!*

I tried diagraming what I wanted to understand just to get it out of my head and on to paper so I might better know it;

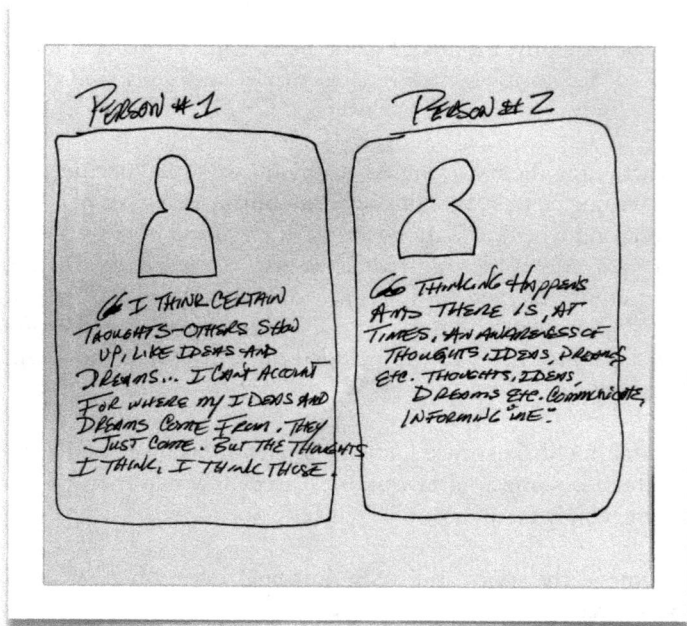

PERSON #1: *I think certain thoughts — others show up, like ideas and dreams . . . I can't account for where my ideas and dreams come from. They just come. But the thoughts I think, I think those.*

(. . . Well who was the "I" thinking that?)

PERSON #2: *Thinking happens and there is, at times, an awareness of thoughts, ideas and dreams, etc. Thoughts, ideas, dreams, etc. communicate, informing "me."*

(. . . That's different.)

It seemed so ridiculous and yet so very important. Once in the research-rabbit-hole it became clear that *thinking is not a verb.* It is not something we ("I") do. Thinking happens. I'm convinced. All that metaphysical stuff; thoughts, ideas, dreams, etc. It shows up in the psyche — the mind — all of it. Period. We don't actually think up any of it, at least not the way we've been taught.

In other words, what if there is no "I," some "central-point-of-You, ego" that chooses, decides, determines, etc. what thoughts to think? What if, instead, thinking is a whole body-mind-spirit system, in action, without "us" lifting a finger?

Then consider that most often we're unaware of our thinking, (or rather, that thinking is even happening), because we're so deeply, viscerally living every thought, idea, dream, etc. and when we're in that, "living every thought" experience, there isn't room for any other reality; possibility.

> I think I better go home.
> I think I'll buy that jacket.
> I think it's going to rain.
> I think I need to check on Cathy.
> I think I'm smarter than the guy over there.
> I think I'll be looking for another job soon.

Well what if we removed the "*I think,*" (which are really two words describing something)?

What remains is . . .
> . . . better go home.
> . . . buy that jacket.
> . . . it's going to rain.
> . . . check on Cathy.
> . . . smarter than the guy over there.
> . . . looking for another job soon.

And that is simply information there, available. No "I" involved — really; which turns out to be a more accurate understanding of how we function, and who we.

And, it's the best news yet; a tipping-point of monumental proportion in understanding who we are and our vast capabilities. Because along with thinking happening, (or information streaming through), so can *an awareness* of all that thinking/information, imagining and dreaming, etc. that's streaming — happen too — when we're taught.

Being aware of my thinking could happen, or being unaware of it could happen too. Seemed pretty black and white to me. The big benefit of being aware of all that streaming-thinking, was . . . *the certain reduction of the stress of it* — every time."

Being aware of the thinking that was happening more often, profoundly reoriented my point-of-view and therefore, my life-outcomes. It felt like some sort of tectonic shift was occurring within, when there was awareness, so that my life was experienced so very differently — very grounded, vivid, unified. It felt as though the center of my identity had been reset to a different position. A more natural, easier center.

So, "thinking happens" emerged as a more accurate understanding than the current accepted belief that each of us is in control of our thoughts, ideas, etc. Or that maybe we're in control of some of our thinking, yet not others, say, dreaming? And where's the borderline to that kind of control? And can we actually follow a thought back to its origin and know why we chose it, out of a vast number of possible, probable thoughts?

If "thinking happens" could be proven and accepted as accurate, and if we were taught thinking actually occurs as a complete body-mind-spirit system continually processing information from the moment we're born (before?), *and that when there is an awareness of the thinking happening, more ideas arise* (is that control?); *that alone,* would profoundly change how we understand ourselves (our identity), how we behave with ourselves and each other (act), and what we create individually and together (innovate).

It would liberate us from an inaccuracy that now breeds extreme fear, *"I'm in control of my thoughts yet why do I keep thinking I'm useless, worthless . . .and life will never change!"*

Right now most of us believe as PERSON #1, that we *think up everything we think, imagine, dream, etc.,* as if thinking is a verb, something we do, some thing that some central-point-of-the-self, ego does — an identity?

And so we identify with thinking as a "doing," and therefore, something we, "can control," and with that belief, we are immediately shackled. The English language keeps the shackles on. Yet suppose it isn't something we "do." Suppose thinking happens and, we, when taught, get to watch all that thinking — unique to each of us, the origin of everything man-made?! And then suppose the watching, yielded more informed, brilliant experiences, ideas, possibilities, than not watching!

It seemed to me if we agreed that "thinking happens" and we taught our children to be aware of all of the thinking happening (that they can tune into) *humanity would suddenly be catapulted into a world of no blame,* and that too, would drive a sea change of biblical proportion. What would *that* be like if we couldn't blame anyone — *not even ourselves* — for anything? Would we self-destruct? Would we thoughtfully innovate? Would we effortlessly care for each other? Would we favorably rewrite our social systems? Would the rest of nature appear more important? Would we all experience our authentic potential?

    "Maybe I'm avoiding it . . . or denying it!"

Well what if our language isn't accurate and you're not doing either of those things?

What if we were all taught that words forming such sentences, was simply, a configuring of language, "thinking at work," connecting, linking information into meaning . . . something our entire body-mind-spirit system constructs and we, can become aware of it? Would that make a difference in our lives, *or in who we think we are?*

Who, or what, was responsible for thinking? Was "responsible" even the right word? Was "driving" a better word? Thoughts like these propelled me to continue probing, and when I reached a tipping-point — where experiencing our full potential depended on a very new understanding of how we function — writing it all down happened, and yes, *I could hardly believe it myself!*

Scientific researchers might say, I was facing a "paradigm crisis" and, I was on my own, as I had no affiliation with any higher education, or research institutions and their many experts. I didn't receive responses to my emails, so my questions remained unanswered by them. I read and watched, and listened to the perspectives that were available, and I saw a different picture associating, emerging, around the process of thinking and how beneficially-extraordinary that picture was — *for everyone of us and the rest of nature too . .*
.

Deep in the rabbit hole I found that two natural attributes — *thinking and observation* — are our species' natural, built-in scales of justice, balancing, ever-processing; providing a way for us to keep ourselves and the rest of what's here, vitally on track. One without the other is a lopsided existence; which can be, in fact, deadly.

Did I "know the subject," how the body-mind-spirit (beyond?) worked — I was finding out. And since the questions had attached themselves so viscerally, following them fervidly, unfolded.

Through his words, the man at the table had given me a gift. He had fueled my fire to know if those natural scales of justice could reign — providing each of us with intrinsic balance.

This way into the information rabbit hole . . .

I considered that what we were taught, learned,
experienced, and know, about ourselves, is really
all in relationship, to something else . . .

3. WHAT WERE WE TAUGHT?

Brains were beginning to appear a bit like books, imprinted with experience, as far as I could tell. Was the brain simply the information-processor for something bigger, say, the mind (the place of information)? Is this a case of hardware (brain), versus software (mind)?

Was the brain and the mind the same? They certainly functioned within the same system.

Going forward, throughout the book, I'll use this combination of words, "brain/mind," prompting the consideration of what they represent. Why two different words? Perhaps we made such a distinction because they do seem to point to separate experiences, yet also overlap.

We say, "Keep your mind on the job." We wouldn't say "Keep your brain on the job." We also say, "Did it ever cross your mind?" Not, "Did it ever cross your brain." We don't say, "Neurons fire in the mind." And the mind is traditionally researched and studied through the field of psychology. We learn about the brain through neuroscience. Yet those fields are beginning to overlap. So I'll use brain/ mind for now, in that I'm imagining them, a collaborative effort that informs us. And for now, let's forget about the location of the "mind". We'll consider "location" in Chapters 8 and 10. We all agree a brain sits in our head.

So, what are your imprinted experiences; what were you taught? It matters. What stories (information) are on the pages of your brain/mind? Do you know?

Out of all of the information you received, what were you not in control of learning, of knowing, or understanding? Was there something you wanted to know, that you didn't discover till much later? With what information are you filled, now, or rather, what information has been imprinted, over time? Do you have *patterns* of thought? What keeps you up at night? What keeps showing up? Ever notice how it matters in relation to the quality of your life experience?

> *"Imagine you had been born to and brought up by a family from another culture living on the other side of the planet. How likely would it be that, that version of you would have the same worldview and behaviors as you do now?"*

That was the question my friend and colleague, asked. He was especially effective at getting me to notice the conceptual stuff that had accrued over a lifetime and continued circulating. We all know the answer to his question with a kind of unsettling feeling . . . *we'd be completely different.*

We learn a language the moment we arrive. We hear variations in voice tone emanating from the mouths of those around us and, we are introduced to meaning. We are taught, *"This* is good. *That* is bad." We are non-verbal at first. We are sensual beings, like radar picking-up moment to moment signals. After we pattern sounds, they are arranged into language and more advanced expression happens. We learn an alphabet, and how to write those symbols (letters) to further express. We learn to tie our shoes and later, how to use a cell phone. We've learned everything we know and what we know becomes patterns over a lifetime; imprints. It's the same for all humans.

Just consider for a moment that everything you know has been taught to you — *everything*. Even taking an online course is a self-taught method in which new information becomes understood. From birth to now, we've absorbed canyons of information.

In following my question, I learned that in the 1980's the neuroscience community revealed we have, in our brains (not in our minds?. . . just had to write that), mirror neuron's. As I understand it, a neuron is basically a cell that transmits information in a specific way . . . Some of these scientists believe these cells activate an ability to mirror-back (thus the name), a gesture, a sound, just about anything (as other animals do), to mimic something toward learning it (patterning). for survival (although it's still under research). Yet mirror neurons, or no mirror neurons, we can and do imitate, we can be shown, taught, where to go, what to do, to wave hello, add numbers, know the days of the week, what's right, wrong (culturally dependent?). The more it becomes a pattern of knowledge, a habit, it's said to be "imprinted." Like a book?

Warlords and how they target children age six, for their armies, was being discussed on a National Public Radio show. I listened intently. The expert explained, *"They prefer them at that age because children so young, 1) are empty of thoughts, 2) seek to please, and 3) are fearless, and therefore easier to fill, to program."* To pattern, mirror . . . to kill?

Brilliant thinking and how horrific as hell that kind of thinking was. Yet, as a mother of two sons, I considered how I filled them with information daily. Then they went off to school and were further "filled." They watched TV programs, movies and read books that continued filling them with information. Their friends filled them, as did their friend's parents. They were filled by the experience of the environment, family, economics, culture, religion, etc. The same thing happened to the rest of us. And, according to where we lived, was the information with which we were filled. The proof of being filled, is what's there in your brain/mind right now and in mine, and his and her's, and all over the Internet and the news, from the brain/minds of others.

We swim in an ocean of information daily which affects everyone – for better or worse. Fake news?

You don't need to research anything to know that between the ages of birth and six years (in utero too?), we're filled with foundational information, and all of that information may become knowledge and perhaps later wisdom or, . . . a detriment to our time here?

After age 10 we are pretty much psychologically, physiologically, and emotionally formed, meaningfully and dramatically, even though we continue to absorb more, and our physical system continues to evolve — even our nose cartilage grows till death!

I was finding out way more than what I was taught about thinking. And I considered that what we were taught, learned, experienced, and know, about ourselves, is really all in relationship, to something else; family, friends, school, work, the sun, wind . . .

That blew my mind.

Sally Kempton, author and spiritual teacher, summed up several of my random thoughts perfectly, *"It's hard to fight an enemy who has outposts in your head."*

Relationships had to be examined . . .

Being human is not a singular act.

4. IN RELATIONSHIP; A MIRRORING?

I had never considered that without oxygen I would cease to exist, or would most likely not exist, as I do. I had lived believing in quite a separate existence; that I only had relationships if I wanted them, or was born into them; father mother, sister, brother.

I came to learn that without the microbial system that comprises our body, the body would cease to function, as-is. Without the flora on earth, and oceanic microbes that produce oxygen, nature as we know it, would be very different. Without the sun, much of the same. Not much of this current life, the kind we're used to, would happen. And without other humans, there would be no procreation, then perhaps no more us. You might say the whole system we call the cosmos, or universe, (whatever word suggests all inclusive), is *interdependent.* Thinking included? Absolutely. How could anything be left out of a complete, living system?!

Being human is not a singular act.

I began to imagine how this might work among us: every actor-celebrity who walked the red carpet . . . They may have felt like a million bucks as they passed throngs of people waving happily, fueling that "million bucks" feeling. Everyone *in relationship;* interdependently experiencing. Yet, if fans were throwing eggs, that "million bucks" feeling might unpredictably snap into fear, anger, or deep sadness (a mirroring?).

"In relationship," seems to be the only way we know ourselves. We exist in relationship to all that's here. Empirical evidence found everywhere. We cannot detach ourselves. That would be only illusion. We even need a mirror to see ourselves and with it, we can't ever see all of ourself . . . at once.

So when a man handed me a deck of "animal medicine cards," I played the game (in relationship). I shuffled, paused, pulled one out, turned it over, and read the words, "*The Chicken*." I smiled, my head tilted slightly and I heard my silent inner-voice say, "*I've never considered Chicken medicine before . . .*" Pleasantly imagining the fortune-telling-possibilities, was happening, until he read the card's "Summary Statement": "*Are you prepared for things to go right?*"

"That's "Chicken medicine?! How nice is that!?" I thought, and in a flash I noticed my delight had vanished . . . all in relationship. The card was a mirror and my system had been triggered, prompted . . . Was it because the "Summary Statement" sounded too good; instantly showing me the imprinted pattern to brace myself in anticipation for things to go wrong!? The pattern that was revealed suddenly, wasn't pretty. Was it taught? Mirrored? How ever it was established, it was in relationship for sure. Why would things going "right," not be my norm?/ Ugh.

Hundreds of thought-dialogues, conversations (and images) in our head, communicating uniquely, are incessant. They play across the sound system within. Ever notice? Is there a "You" thinking all that up? What part(s) of "You" would be doing that?

I read somewhere that 70% of what's there in, or on our brain/minds, for most of us, is negative. Is that possible (how do we test for that)? *That's painful!* As I kept investigating, a whole group of *painful thoughts* showed up. They sounded like this . . .

> *"What if I don't remember!? What if I forget the stuff I've written down?! What if there's stuff I don't even know, that I should know, and remember, what about that stuff!? . . . I'm f**k'd!"*

Where was that kind of thinking headed?

Thoughts can escalate. I kept listening . . .
> *"Do you really want to think that . . . again!"*
> *"You're really going to go there — again?*

Then they shifted . . .
> *"Well if you don't like it, then think of something else!"*
Followed by,
> *"Who is the You, You are speaking to?!*
And then . . .
> *"OMG!" My mind is arguing with itself!"*

You can't make this stuff up! (Boy did that ever have new meaning.)

Is there really an "I" that selects all the thoughts I hear within, really? — all of those past and future thoughts, ideas, dreams, dialogue processing every moment, from all the information absorbed every second, over a lifetime?!

Do we really, deliberately change our focus almost every minute, in relationship to all of it?! Or, am I more than who I think I am? Is there more to me than originally thought, known, taught?

If there really is an "I," some central-point of "Me" that "chooses" the "thoughts, daydreams . . ." when awake, and let's say, not my "night dreams" when sleeping, then what part of "Me" sorts out and "chooses" which thinking and dreaming happens when, determining which will be my experience at the moment?! It mattered! There was a lot at stake . . . Are you following the thinking?

When you read or hear the word "reward," what arises in your mind? How does your body respond? How about the word, "punishment" and is your response to that word the same, each time? What thoughts *surface* when reading the stock market figures, or watching global news, finding out your team won the Super Bowl, or reading Bitcoin hit $20k? . . . Why those thoughts? What's the relationship?

What we were taught is in relationship to the rest of what's here — air, water, food, protests, your cat, or grandmother, culture, thunderstorms, birthdays, time, and so on. Turns out nothing is independent, as we may have believed, not you, not me . . .

It seemed as if every thought could be a reward, or punishment . . . Freedom or captivity . . . and I could know, if I paid attention . . .

When we were young we had adults show us what to pay attention to, and do, and what not to do. Now we need to find new ways of educating ourselves, prompting the full ebb and flow of all of our attributes. In doing so, we get to establish new relationships and patterns ensuring that observation (paying attention) is a primary sense ability, fully active, grounding us, balancing us, reducing hostility within.

So let's practice observing relationships . . .

Read through Prompt beginning on the next page, then put the book down and for 3-minutes really consider, and pay attention to the information that's noticed . . .

PROMPT #1:

IN RELATIONSHIP: Set a timer for 3-minutes . . .

Begin to consider that you are in relationship to all that's here . . .

Notice (observe) that you are in relationship to everything, and that everything comes right up to your skin. Imagine that the light waves your eyes can and can't see, and sound waves that your ears can and can't hear, are touching you, penetrating you, moving past and around you.

Notice the air that's there. Can you feel it against your skin? Is it windy? Are you inside, with the heat on? No matter how subtle, become aware of your relationship to it . . .

Also consider that there is no such thing as empty space and that something, many "things" are there, all around you . . .

Now notice how gravity supports your feet and the rest of your body in connecting with the ground so you may walk, run, stand on your tip-toes . . . Without it, would you be weightless, floating, experiencing a very different sense of life?

Now take notice of the aliveness of the plant you might water weekly, the buildings outside, the creatures — insects to mammals — included in your environment and just consider being in-relationship to all that, as if the space around you — 360 degrees — was filled and alive with stuff in flux; the unseen and the seen, the natural humming of nature — your heartbeat included.

Finally notice what your body is doing in relationship to everything. Is it content, relaxed, fearful, tense?

Step into that "relationship experience" on and off for the rest of the day, and observe what appears to your senses (antenna?).

And, if we considered that a relationship can be known as a dynamic pattern of stuff, happening, interacting, in ebb and flow, we might then see that there are dynamic flows of patterns everywhere.

And, since we are an aspect of what's here, we come equipped with patterns; we are a catalyst for patterns to happen; individually and en masse.

Then I landed on Goethe's missive, *"The One brings many out of itself,"* and it seemed to make the idea of patterns clearer . . . Following them happened next . . .

Is the brain/mind only as useful as the information it absorbs?
Is this a hostage situation?!

5. PATTERN POWER . . .

In the rabbit hole I learned that most scientists now agree
there is vibration, flow, rhythm to everything — *everything*
— that nothing is actually still (motionless), and that those
vibrations are patterns. Iterations.

Patterns (e.g., repeated marks, colors, placement, etc.) reveal
themselves in our DNA, in and on our skin, in plant and rock
structure, in planetary movement, music, weather,
reproduction, thoughts, dance, communication, the seasons,
you name it! Patterns have kept us alive, or killed us, (think
heroism, homicide, earthquakes, climate change?) . . . Again,
empirical evidence . . . all we have to do is look around. Are
they mirrored?

I had seen the Mandelbrot set; hypnotically stunning, visual
patterns, computer programed, ". . . *by iterating a simple algebraic*
expression . . ." (*Turbulent Mirror*, J.Briggs, F.D.Peat). The key
word here being, "iterating." Turned out, iteration produced a
most mind-blowing visual pattern and, it was "bottomless,"
infinite! It's worth it to see those natural powerful-patterns;
search online, "Mandelbrot set".

I had never been prompted to notice patterns — until I was
in up to my knees in, thinking about thinking . . . What a
pattern!

At times we don't keep promises, commitments, resolutions and that pattern surprises us. We can't seem to be on time and that pattern frustrates us. We can be forgetful, unprepared or, we ". . . *aren't thinking straight,*" a phrase created to communicate the experience of, "I don't know why I'm thinking that, again . . . when I'd prefer to be thinking something else!"

We were all taught, and accepted, (maybe without our awareness, or choosing) , that we are responsible for what we think, and do. Yet I believe, that understanding hasn't helped us answer questions like, "Why do I get blindsided?" "Why didn't I see that coming; the car, the divorce, the suicide, getting fired, hired, the pregnancy, the surprise party . . . if I'm in control of my thoughts and actions?!"

If we're in control, why can't we just, "let go, stop it, change our minds, release our resentments, forgive, shape up, or open our hearts," on command?! And, why can't we, more often than not, "just do it!"!? And why do we snap to extremes?! Do we intend to?

We've been told, "choose what's best", "intend your dreams", "set goals", "decide", "be responsible," and, "don't avoid . . ." and then our actions reveal otherwise and we're completely stumped. We blame ourselves, our thinking and actions, believing we've "lost control." We had it . . . then lost it. How did we do that? I thought we were in control.

We say,
> "*What's wrong with me!?*", "*Why can't I just remember, make up my mind, stop worrying, and know what to do next?!*", "*Why am I still making bad decisions?!*," "*It wasn't my intention!,*" "*I didn't mean to!*"

Well . . . what if we couldn't know, or never had control, to be able to do any of that, on demand — in the way we were taught to understand that we did? Long question. (Is there a pattern here?)

What if we only "have control" and "choice," if we were taught to think, believe, we do?

We learned and believed, and patterns formed. Every morning we arose and brushed our teeth. Every day we expected . . . the best . . . the worst? Was that a pattern, dependent on what was happening all around; triggering responses?

Was it reasonable to consider that our responses were patterns showing us what we had absorbed; an aversion to this, an attraction to that . . . if only we were directed to pay attention?

Stanley I. Greenspan, M.D., and Stuart, G. Shanker, D.PHIL, in their book, *The first Idea*, seemed to back me without knowing it, *"Fear . . . is no longer a single emotion but part of an interactive pattern."*

With instruction, so is our life? Does it matter — the iterations?! What do you think?

On my reading list was Dr. Robert Sapolsky's 2017 book, *Behave: The Biology of Humans at Our Best and Worst.* Sapolsky, a neuroendocrinologist and a professor of biology and neurology and neurological sciences at Stanford University noted: *"Adolescence shows us that the most interesting part of the brain evolved to be shaped minimally by genes and maximally by experience; that's how we learn —context, context, context."* It was incredible to me that a scientist believed that how we are "shaped" is less about "genes" and more about "context" — *experience!* And isn't experience patterns of relationship?

Sapolsky's book also offered an understanding of the intertwining of physiology, biology and belief — when it comes to our "best and worst" behavior. There doesn't seem to exist any singular, separate, aspect from where our best and worst expressions emerge! "Context was a big sandbox. Environment included, all of it together, physiology, biology, belief — all in relationship, since the beginning of time, producing experience. Inseparable!

So . . . what part of that did "You" and "I" control? (The damn question again.)

Is the brain/mind only as useful as the information it absorbs? Is this a hostage situation?!

I wondered if absorbing information would matter more to each of us, if that was in fact the case. Just like what we eat matters to our body, does our pattern of thought (belief, understanding) mess with our bodies too? Do we snap into violence from patterns of bad thinking, information poisoning, sickening beliefs, or into insight, from absorbing information that's life affirming?

What stimulates the vast probable thoughts within? What might make you snap toward either end of the emotional spectrum and why?

> I hear silently, *"Do you know your patterns — the details? . . . You're not going to notice them just once. It's on-going. You're ever-growing and changing. It's an iteration-evolution.*
>
> *. . . And if there's awareness about the evolution, all those patterns — OMG! — what a cool "context" to live in!"*

I had lots of "what" questions . . . What was patterning made of; repetition of what exactly, and what set it in motion?

Maybe observing some patterns, yours, their's and nature's, would offer some answers?

Let's practice observing patterns . . .

PROMPT #2:

PATTERNS IN MOTION: Consider that you are a pattern in motion: **A, B, C, D, E**

> **A:** Do you find yourself checking the time often? Do you wash your hands regularly? Do you check a to-do list, or always prep your coffee maker before going to sleep? Do you meditate each morning, maybe before a daily shower? Is there a pattern there?
>
> You may be aware, that in the morning you wake up, wash up, have your cup of coffee, then feed and walk the dog . . . What patterns are you aware of about yourself, your life? How about your heartbeat? Your breathing? Is it comfortable, uncomfortable?
>
> What same thought and/or action happens often? Are the same words spoken during similar experiences? Do you get sick the same time, each year? Observe your patterns . . . of thinking, feeling, speaking, relating . . . What's there?
>
> **B:** Next observe the patterns of others; your friends, colleagues, parents, partner, kids, boss, teacher, politicians . . . What do you notice? Are you aware that you like some of their patterns and not others?
>
> **C:** How about patterns in nature? Clouds, mountains, a leaf, the pattern in your dog's fur. What do you notice about nature, the seasons, its colors, textures, temperature, smells, and feel of it? Does if feel balanced, unbalanced?

D: Draw or paint a few patterns. Dance a pattern, sing a pattern of lyrics, rhythm or melody. See what shows up when deliberately expressing patterns?

E: What occurs when there is an awareness of patterns all around; on you, in you? How about if you consider that you're adding your patterns to a larger universal pattern; the planets in orbit . . . ?

Oh the beauty of patterns, or not . . . a tsunami, a repeated abusive thought?

Were prompts, triggers and stimuli involved in creating patterns? Were *they* patterns?

Do I absorb information whether I want to or not?

6. PROMPTS, TRIGGERS & STIMULI — OH MY!

Ebb and flow. Left, right. The pendulum swings . . . it goes this way, and that. Attraction, repulsion. Information in motion? Associations happening? Patterns? Dots were connecting.

Consider a time when you were learning to put on your pants, ride a bike, do the math, or socialize. Someone was there teaching you, prompting you on what to do, to stay on track and "get it," so you'd be able to do it over and over and over, without them. Maybe a grandparent, teacher, guardian, or friend, corrected you until something was mastered. You watched others and that prompted you; as did the weather, TV, what you ate, fresh air . . . all of it triggered responses making patterns . . . ?

> . . . I'm dressed, ready to go. I hear unexpected rain outside and I notice the image of an umbrella on the maxi-screen in my brain/mind. I find myself getting an umbrella before going to the door . . .

Interesting. Hearing the rain prompted an image of an umbrella, then the action to get it followed . . . Was that ever smooth! . . . A learned pattern, an association of care?

I considered prompts, and how many of my patterns go unnoticed . . .

No question we're all in relationship to billions of data bits that stimulate response — every moment we've been alive. Incredible when you consider it. I imagined that everything from feeling heat to receiving praise (the red carpet?) prompted our systems to respond uniquely; and our systems have been responding, reacting, experiencing uniquely — ever since.

Prompt, response, prompt, response, a pattern of existence unfolding, multiplying itself, pollinating, informing, forming . . . electrical and chemical reactions happening in the brain. I found out we have the 2000 Nobel Prize-winning American Neuroscientist, Dr. Paul Greengard to thank for the research showing that, "electrical and chemical signaling worked in tandem in the brain." Remarkable patterns in motion? (NYT, April 15, 2019.) Life happening. Thinking included, happening? It never stops.

So, if thinking consists of electrical and chemical signaling — patterns of information — informing us (a whole body-brain/mind-spirit system processing), and not something we "control," we could think we were all, under the influence of information, (just a matter of what, or whose; Warlords?), until we aren't; when we can become aware of the information there (which instantly changes a pattern).

We're all prompted (influenced, triggered), by terrorism and acts of kindness. We prompt each other daily with every word that flows from our mouths, or from social media, loud speakers, and so on.

"Basically, information is experience." wrote, Jane Roberts and Robert F. Butts, in their book, *The Nature of the Psyche.*

The next time I turned on the radio, there was an awareness of my system's response to what it heard. I realized radio programming is highly influential. Usually something else is being done while listening, such as driving, or using my computer. Radio in the background, the information, music, lyrics, commercials, etc., is heard in a kind of hypnotic state; information imprinting patterns on my brain/mind, while I'm not noticing, or rather focused elsewhere? *Do I absorb information whether I want to or not?* UGH! (Interesting that bothered me.)

What we hear, see . . . sense matters. Our systems create associations of information. Linking, linking, linking . . .

What is your radio dial, YouTube channel, Instagram tuned to, and do those patterns of information positively fill you, (with loving associations)? What are you agreeing to listen to? Is that by choice? And what are you responding to? Mirroring? What associations are happening? What's prompting you? . . .

I absorbed that the brain/mind doesn't act alone in any processing it does. It requires the rest of the system — body, sunlight, oceans, anniversaries, etc. — all in a relationship (patterns for sure).

We also now know, that our ability to sense, (that unique triggered-response of each of our senses), is in direct relationship to prompts, and that everything is a prompt . . . including the words on this page, as they provide unique associations from you, as you read along. Is there an "I" choosing them? Or is your system JUST responding?

I've been wanting to send a letter to most of the major newspapers and news channels in the USA . . .
> "Please, stop publishing patterns of horrific headlines . . . The headlines you're agreeing to issue are assisting in prompting a health epidemic of epic proportion — a trigger for extreme fear. And, if you're using painful associations to sell your brand, WTF!?! . . . *You know we all feel the news.* Generate solutions to strengthen the intrinsic vitality and global-

health of people! Instead pattern headlines to develop curiosity, and associate win-win possibilities, versus perpetuate fear and hate . . . It matters!"

Sensing new associations was triggered . . .

Does a whole, alive system, control itself?!

7. SENSE ABILITY:
IT'S ONLY NATURAL

I kept the *New Scientist* magazine, because the January 29-February 4, 2005 issue's cover story was, *"Why you have at least 21 senses."* Twenty-one was way up from the basic five I was taught; seeing, hearing, tasting, smelling, and touching, (and is touching different from feeling, and with what sense do we feel weight, physically, emotionally?!) I was excited to find out. The senses had shown up, fueling my understanding of the questions, 1) did I control my thoughts, and, 2) could I reduce the occurrence of the painful ones (liberating me into a balanced life)? I could *feel* the senses were woven into thinking . . .

"How many senses DO we have?" was a report posted in November 2014, on the BBC's (British Broadcasting Corporation) website based on a chapter from Christian Jarrett's new book, *Great Myths of the Brain,* (Wiley), which moved me forward.

> "Simply defining what we mean by a 'sense' leads you down a slippery slope into philosophy. One, somewhat vague, definition might argue that a human sense is simply a unique way for the brain to receive information about the world and the body. If that is the case, then we can claim with confidence that there are certainly more than five human senses."

There seemed further evidence that there may be countless ways we "receive information," and not so much that we actually, *think it all up*.

> "As you can see, there is no single, logical way to define the senses. In some ways, it might make little sense to draw divisions between them at all – considering that they often seem to blend together . . ."

In that same article Jarrett links to a September 2012, *New Scientist* article By Jan Westerhoff, titled, *"Reality: The definition"*. His opening paragraph,

> *"What do we actually mean by reality?"*

Stick with me . . .

> "A straightforward answer is that it means everything that appears to our . . . senses — everything that we can see, smell, touch and so forth. Yet this answer ignores such problematic entities as electrons, the recession and the number 5, . . . which are very real. It also ignores phantom limbs and illusory smells. Both can appear vividly real…"

So what does *reality* have to do with the process of thinking?! . . .

In his 2011 book, *The Compass of Pleasure*, neurobiologist, David J. Linden of John's Hopkins University, revealed how the, *"reward system" in our brain*, (a region also called by some as the "pleasure center," since researchers have watched chemical and electrical firing intensify at that location during pleasurable experiences), does not distinguish between reality and non-reality (No such thing as fantasy — *it's all real?!).* The brain is simply, always, processing information. *What?!* Everything is "real" to the brain?! This gets even more crazy-dicey if you're steadfast on believing you're in control of your thinking (and would that mean, in control of your brain, mind, both — and all that firing included?); a belief that was beginning to completely fade as fact, for me. And, at this moment in history, we just don't know yet. We're beginning to understand . . . I was feeling like a part of that movement.

Every sense ability (and yes, two words) we have, stimulates brain/mind activity; prompt, response, or maybe it's simultaneous? Our senses, no matter the number — are our radar, sonar, probes, antenna, to knowing all that surrounds us. Like the whiskers of a cat, they inform. Is it safe, too heavy, too loud, not sweet enough . . . ? Our senses seem to guide us, sending and receiving responding to prompts, stimulation — and as naturally as breathing . . .

The stuff we do know, about how we work, blows my mind . . .

Even *Humans of New York,* posted this short dialogue along with a photo of two eye doctors sitting on a bench, on June 6, 2014:

> *"We're eye doctors."*
> *"What's something about the eye that most people don't realize?"*
> *"The eye doesn't see. The brain sees. The eye just transmits. So what we see isn't only determined by what comes through the eyes. What we see is affected by our memories, our feelings, and by what we've seen before."*

Our eyes don't see?! OMG! And what we see is "affected by memories and feelings" . . . ! That's not what I was taught.

Sight, our most used sense, occurs even with our eyes closed (sighted or unsighted). So when the sight of something happens, and the entire system believes what it sees is dangerous, (eyes open, or closed; dreams?), the brain's amygdala is triggered, which triggers the release of hormones and steroids (from the adrenal glands), such as adrenaline, cortisol, aldosterone, and testosterone. The adrenal glands also regulate blood pressure, metabolism, responses to fear, and the immune system; triggering the rest of the system into action (fight, flight), to a complete halt (freeze), or into submission (fawn).

Does a whole, alive system, control itself?!

Just imagine a sound, scent, flavor, or the feeling of something and then snapping into an extreme expression . . .?

> "I just had it in my hand! Where did I put it, if I was holding it?" Such thoughts were distressing my whole system. I had to go! I wanted to be on time! I was beginning to sweat . . . I would have sworn in a court of law, that I had brought it with me. Yet where was it? The visual in my mind, of holding it in my hand, the feeling of it against my fingers, was so real! Where the heck did I put it?! I would have sworn on a visual in my head, a feeling in my hand, a sense, (a memory, an imagination?), that I had put it somewhere and, I would have been wrong — maybe partially. The phone was still charging, plugged into the outlet downstairs.

Every thought has a physical response that accompanies it. I call that, emotion. I share more about emotions in Chapter 9. For now, ever notice the inter-weaving of your physiological functions and thoughts? Or that the unpredictability of an experience can be . . . sensibly-alarming!? Recall the surprise party, or the intensity of, *"It wasn't my intention!", "I didn't mean to!"*

It was becoming clear that like a gene, senses can be triggered, snapping into expression of chemical and electric currents, gyrating in every direction, body-wide, brain/

mind-wide, emotion-wide; inextricably mixed with environment — and the whole Universe?

I found this enlightening wisdom, in Tamarack Song's book, *Becoming Nature*, "*Animal Mind . . . has more to do with sensing the rhythms . . .* "

So what did I now understand? Information, whether a breeze or a thought, prompts our entire system to naturally broadcast a spectrum of vibrational-intensities, rhythms, patterns — *which can be known*; even when walking across a fog-covered bridge at dusk (Mother Teresa) . . .

Was my system managing my wellbeing without "me" — assisting, already prioritizing for my benefit? Was that accurate?

If every response that happens is our system at work (processing), navigating its way to safety, steadiness, security, joy, anger . . . according to what we've absorbed; then it could be said that every cell we are comprised of, is collaboratively offering information to the entire system; and those intensities we feel, taste, smell . . . let us know what's happening if, we're paying attention . . .

A seashell shaped Madeline cookie conjured childhood memories for Marcel Proust, who wrote extensively about such a perplexing occurrence in his novel, *Remembrance of Things Past* (which was later re-named, *In Search of Lost Time*). Proust smelled and then bit into a freshly baked cookie and experiences he hadn't felt, seen, heard, tasted, nor smelled in decades, flooded him. It was so profound, he became obsessed with understanding the brain and how it operated; weaving images, stories and meaning from the smell and taste of a cookie (the trigger?). In a moment he had an unpredictably intense experience. Had he snapped into something . . . good?

Was every sound, smell, taste, touch, sight of something a catalyst for thinking to happen?

One Sunday morning I sent the following text message to my sister, regarding my youngest son, who was 25:

(In my txt script.)

"He was invited to a surprise BDay party a girl is giving for her boyfriend n they're all going skydiving at 4PM. How is ur day unfolding? :)"

Ok, so I was beginning to learn that at a micro level, I'm an alive network of electrical and chemical responses to stimuli. Ok! So, was knowing that my son was going to jump from an airplane at 4PM, for the fun of it, the catalyst of the low-grade fearful thoughts and slight nausea that was vibrating through me . . .?

Are instantaneous thoughts and their patterns, the culprit of our delight or pain, imprisonment or liberation? None of our own choosing? And can patterns be altered, or eliminated? How?

With every phone call, email, drink swallowed, if attention was paid to our responses, might that drive better decisions and outcomes? Thinking was broadcasting questions . . .

Here's a long one — if from birth we were all taught that;

- at our core, we are vital electrical and chemical responses happening, 24/7
- our whole system, head to toe, is processing, evaluating prioritizing — setting intensities for all that incoming information — for our wellbeing
- action happens like thinking happens
- we can be aware of actions and thinking
- we can be aware of another's actions and thinking simply by hearing their words, by reading what they've written, or listening to the music they've made, by eating the food they cook . . . by watching them, etc.

- we can be aware of feeling, hearing, tasting, etc., as well as learning the alphabet, numbers, good/bad, and so on
- we are in relationship to larger systems; air, water, shopping malls, rainbows, accidents, which we deeply experience — joy to pain

. . . do you suppose with the patterning of those kinds of understandings, our experience here might be positively different?

Ever feel the hair stand up on the back of your neck, forearms, or shoulders? Ever wince at a harsh sound? Ever burst out laughing while watching a favorite show? Or hold your nose so you can't smell foul air? At their core, aren't they electrical and chemical responses happening? Does knowing that make any difference to your sense ability, and sense of identity, who you believe you are?

And with the awareness of our thinking and actions patterned also, would that make a huge improvement in our emotional lives? I think it would. What do you think?

If we believe we control our thinking, *(electrical and chemical responses too),* that former pattern that's heard in your head remains:

> "What if I don't remember!? What if I forget the stuff I've written down?! What if there's stuff I don't even know, that I should know and remember, what about that stuff!? . . .

However, if there is a "whole-system-You" that is controlling — choosing, sorting thoughts — a new pattern of understanding who you are, with a fuller awareness of all sense abilities, etc., might sound something like this:

> *"I'm aware of the thoughts, "What if I don't remember!? What if I forget the stuff yadayadayada. . . . ?" I'm also aware of how my body feels in relationship to those*

thoughts. It doesn't feel good . . . Well . . . What else is possible?"

Hold that example in mind. It will come up again, (Chapter 11) consolidated. I promise . . . *can I even do that?*

Now is a good time to practice a sensible Prompt . . .

There are lots of sensing practices out there that will support you in heightening your sense-experience. For now, play with Prompt #3.

Again, read it through, then put the book down and for 3-minutes really pay attention to you . . .

PROMPT #3:
WHAT ARE YOU SENSING?: Scan your 21+ . . .

Consider that you are big data walking . . . What's being sensed right now, by your 21+ sense abilities? What information (data) is registering on your radar?

Sitting or standing, pause, close your eyes, inhale deeply, exhale fully and comfortably, 3x's. (Closing your eyes may feel awkward at first, no matter where you are. It may be because it's something you don't do often, while awake. Yet closing your eyes heightens the rest of your sensory perceptions . . .)

So, breathing deeply and easily, with eyes closed, taking three deep invigorating breaths, really track the air being brought into your system, and then leaving it, in other words, pay attention to where the air is going, what's happening when breathing is ocurring.

Then, with eyes still closed start scanning your feet and move up to the top of your head, slowly noticing what's happening there. What do you feel? Scan every inch. Notice the details. That's the goal.

Now sense with your eyes still closed, as if you were *inside* your body, your thumb, hips, chest, lungs, mouth, organs. . . experiencing them intimately.

Then, open your eyes, and take a moment to scan every inch of your body — again, toes to head (or the other way around if you like).

What's happening with the heels of your feet, ankles, knees, your left pinky finger, stomach, heartbeat, upper back, shoulders, right ear, groin, neck . . . Then again, get inside your body and observe with eyes open. Is there stiffness, aches, butterflies, a sweet taste, a heaviness, something else . . .? Is there heat, cold, an itchiness, prickliness present; muscles tight, soft?

As you take notice, with eyes closed and open, and you become aware of what's happening throughout your entire body, then move your awareness to what's around you, your environment — 360°. Slowly turn around, if you like, as you take in — receive — what's there. What do you see, hear, taste . . . ? How does your body feel in relationship to what's there? Warm, wet, weak? What are you picking-up? Do you have goose bumps? How are your senses responding? You can know!

I was aware of sensing and thinking happening, more than ever . . . Wanting more information kept happening too. Was that my brain/mind craving information?

There is something about being aware of a thought
(or anything), that profoundly changes . . . everything.

8. BRAIN/MIND?
COMMUNICATING ALONG WITH
THE SENSES?

"The monkeys (and presumably humans as well), are getting a
pleasure buzz from information." was also in David J. Linden's
book, *The Compass of Pleasure.* What!? So what's that mean
to me, to us? It means I, we the people, (like monkeys),
know we love information (monkey mind?). Information is
indeed, pollen for the mind and we can transform data and
information into knowledge, and even wisdom (the
honey?), over a lifetime. We are "big data" walking! We
love to know. And I was taught that knowing was good,
and not knowing was, well, not so good . . .

Growing up I was often asked, *"How are you going to do that?"*
Sometimes the "how" was clear and sometimes it was
completely absent. So when I didn't know the "how" of
"doing," my body would get tense and cranky. Knowing
"how" seemed as if one had the key, or a kind of superhero
ability to *control* something, anything . . . maybe
everything . . . and, I should know how to do that . . .
because I'm in control — right?!

I wasn't taught to be at ease with not knowing, or that not
knowing was in fact, an aspect of the process of knowing. I
had little mirroring for that? My flavor of not knowing lead
to fear — of living, (*"What if I don't remember . . . !"* sound

familiar?). Again, my body would get tense and cranky (restricted from a balanced ebb and flow). Recall, "Every thought has a physical response that accompanies it" . . . That was a pattern learned quite young and it affected and effected all aspects of my life, until, it didn't . . . as much.

Ok, so we humans love information. We inhale content online feeling every word read, and visual seen, as it sparks some kind of ecstatic satisfaction all over, and so we keep reading, watching and listening. We want to know. Information tells us who we are, and how we . . . should be? And apparently now, it's proven that we get a *"pleasure buzz"* from it — even the horrific.

We come equipped to experience vast expression, as we absorb information — 360. Our Myths, contemporary stories, social media, etc., offer much detail of the depths and heights we can experience; we can become Mother Teresa, or a suicide bomber, depending on what's been imprinted on/in(?) our brain/mind.

Is information addicting?

In the book *WICKED: The life and times of the Wicked Witch of the West*, (think Wizard of Oz), author Gregory Maguire tells the back-story of how she became hateful and cruel, revealing she wasn't always "wicked," and was certainly not born that way.

The book was made into a Tony Award-winning Broadway musical and one of the most gut-wrenching songs performed by Elfaba (the Wicked Witch of the West) and Glinda (the Good Witch of the East) begins with Elfaba's simple suffering . . .

> "I'm limited.
> Just look at me. (Elfaba was born green.)
> I'm limited.
> And just look at you.

You can do all I couldn't do." (Glinda, Witch of the East, was born a beauty.)

Seems we are all poised to be Elfabas, having the potential to become something we never imagined we would be – deadly cruel? Do we plan that?

We naturally want to know, and at some point we naturally want to know we are good ("*I didn't shove the knife through...*"). With "Elfaba-thinking" (because of what's been imprinted), we don't know we are good. Instead we believe green skin is bad, ugly, and so life unfolds. We become as bad and ugly as we know our skin to be — or not. It can unfold either way. It's unpredictable, which is why, being aware of what's there, *what's been absorbed*, matters. Loving saintliness to murderous rage . . . we can express it all. And we do.

So what happens to those of us who are experiencing an exceptionally hurtful thought, with an intensely vile response surging through our system? With all that biological electrical and chemical eruption happening, *without any awareness of what's being thought and sensed*, at that moment, *when we are in it* — we are painfully snapping.

Without awareness of what's happening at *those* moments, what we are experiencing will be our only *reality*. Until it isn't. Due to some new prompt, trigger, stimuli.

Ever notice that?

If joy, however, is the end of the spectrum we've snapped into, even without knowing snapping has happened, joy is still joy, feeling way better than rage or grief. Both experiences, quite different, yet the same — an unawareness there.

You may know the American Cherokee Indian folktale, *Two Wolves*, wherein an elder Cherokee is teaching his grandson about life. "A fighting is going on inside me," he said to the boy. It is a terrible fight and it is between two wolves. One is evil — he is anger, envy, sorrow, regret, greed, arrogance, self-pity, guilt, resentment, inferiority, lies, false pride, superiority, and ego." He continued, "The other is good — he is joy, peace, love, hope, serenity, humility, kindness, benevolence, empathy, generosity, truth, compassion, and faith. The same fight is going on inside of you – and inside every other person, too." The grandson thought about it and then asked his grandfather, "Which wolf will win?" The Elder simply replied, "The one you feed."

Do we control which is being fed? Would being aware of "the wolves" control and balance them?

Various religions show references to the, "Angel and Devil" (our best and worst thinking and behavior), perched on each shoulder advising us. Some of us know these opposites well, and it seems to me that depending on how quickly we become aware of those, "Angel / Devil" voices, we are *hearing, (sensing, experiencing)* feeding(?), will determine how long the "feeding" lasts . . .

> *Things are seldom what they seem,*
> *Skim milk masquerading as cream,*
> *Externals don't portray insides,*
> *Jekylls may be masking Hydes.*
> – Mr. Jones

There is something about being aware of a thought (or anything), that profoundly changes . . . everything.

In his 1886 groundbreaking novella, *The Strange Case of Dr. Jekyll and Mr. Hyde*, Robert Louis Stevenson gave voice to such behavioral extremes, as well as the act of snapping. Stevenson was captivated by the human capacity for acute expression, and created Dr. Jekyll as the caring-healer, while Mr. Hyde was the violent murderer (the naturally erratic, potential terrorist within?). We find out in the middle of the story that Jekyll and Hyde are one and the same. From this Stevenson weaves a masterful commentary on human unpredictability and *"Jekyll and Hyde"* morphs into a mainstream phrase that conveys someone with an intensely alternating personality — snapping for sure, *"He's so Jekyll/Hyde!"*

There was something else I found in the rabbit hole of research, that was stunning . . . In the book, *Why We Snap*, pages 263/4, by R. Douglas Fields, Ph.D., a senior investigator at the National Institutes of Health, revealed an experiment that neuroscientist David Anderson of Caltech and his research team, had been doing with mice, by way of optogenetics, *"which allows activity in individual neurons [in the brain] to be turned on or off by light stimulation."* The mice were equipped for testing and the research began . . .

> *"Each time an intense blue light was switched on, to activate the neurons. . . the mice began to fight. The battles ceased, when the laser light was switched off . . ."*

Dr. Anderson and his team went even further. Instead of, *"blasting the neurons with a strong laser beam"* they simply turned the light up slow, *"like turning up a dimmer switch."* What they found was,

> *"the exact <u>same neurons that caused fighting now caused mating</u> . . . So <u>the same neurons</u> . . . <u>control both violence and sex . . ."</u>*
> [My underline.]

Wow wee! If blasted, they fight. Slow things down (lessen the intensity) and they mate!? What is it about the quick or gradual intensity of the light? Could this "quick or gradual intensity apply to any system"

Can I *control* the activity of my neurons?! OMG! Can I control the response to prompts, triggers, associations? No matter how quick or gradual?

Elfaba, Jekyll/Hyde, the Two Wolves, Angel/Devil, no matter the label, we have a vast, natural spectrum of expression, and intensities. To recognize and learn our unique and individual spectrum of responses to stimuli, say, even to light (sunlight, fluorescent bulbs, the multi-flashing lights of a police car, or tow-truck on the highway, at night . . . ?), seemed crucial to our overall wellbeing individually and as a whole humanity.

So here's a brain/mind Prompt . . .   Once again read through, it, then put down the book and experience it . . .

PROMPT #4:
JEKYLL/HYDE: A meeting of your Minds.

> Sitting or standing, pause, close your eyes,   inhale deeply, exhale fully and comfortably. 3x's with eyes closed. By now you know the pattern.
>
> Now with eyes remaining closed, create, visualize, and imagine, that an emotional-spectrum in the form of a line, showing rage to saintliness, is about 10 feet in front of you, stretching left to right.
>
> Rage, or the equivalent of extreme violence is at the very left of the line, and Saintliness, or the equivalent of love is to the extreme right.
>
> Now take a moment to see, hear, feel, smell, etc.; with all of your sense ability, the possible variations of that emotional-spectrum, left to right, and vice versa. The middle of the line is neutral — a place of balance.

Now imagine that there is a mini-you standing at each end of this projected emotion-spectrum; there is a mini-you at the far left and a mini-you at the far right. (You may draw this too, if that helps to experience it.) Take a moment and scan the spectrum to viscerally sense some of what's possible with the mini-you to the left, as well as the one to the far right. We all come equipped to experience the entire emotional spectrum.

Now in your imagination, observe, as each mini-you begins to slowly walk toward the center of the spectrum, toward balance. Continue to watch both of them, as they meet in the middle — at the most neutral place of emotion — at the balanced center.

Then observe as your mini-you's look at each other and shake hands, acknowledging each other (or maybe they nod, or bow in acknowledgement); accepting each other's existence, knowing what each is capable of expressing.

Observe them individually, and their relationship. Observe how your body and brain/mind respond to them, their meeting and acknowledgement. When you feel you've fully experienced your Jekyll/Hyde and their meeting, take a deep breath, open your eyes and return to your present space.

Getting to know your Jekyll/Hyde is a real eye-opener, and a fast-track to setting observation in motion. Repeat this visualization often.

"Did I know my Jekyll/Hyde?" At that moment there was an awareness of the question and, it was highly emotional . . .

Ah yes — emotions . . .

Is a legacy understanding "that just ain't so," limiting us . . . ?

9. EMOTION:
BODY & BRAIN/MIND TOGETHER?

Daniel Kahneman, 2002 Nobel Memorial Prize-winner in Economic Sciences, wrote the book, *Thinking Fast and Slow (2011),* and there on p.24 I read,

> *". . . System 1 runs automatically and System 2 is normally in a comfortable, low-effort mode, in which only a fraction of its capacity is engaged . . ."* The, "Systems . . . *two systems in the mind" (fast and slow thinking) . . . researchers have been considering for ages."*

I wondered if, throughout the book, System 1 (S1) — thinking fast — might compare to being "in it," in an experience, and so it was all happening quickly (like being in "the zone"?), and if System 2 (S2) — slow thinking — might be compared to observing all that "fast" stuff, taking its time, paying attention . . .

And then I wondered, who, or what was/is in charge of both "Systems" — the "automatic" and "low-effort mode," setting them in motion? I kept reading . . .

Yet no matter the velocity of thinking, the intensity of the stimuli, nor the spectrum of response experienced, does the act of emotionally snapping begin earlier in life as Dr. Sapolsky outlined, and not in our DNA? Is snap-thinking a natural knee-jerk response like instantly buttoning your coat when a cold wind whips up (S1)? Is it like coughing, or sneezing — simply a response to stimuli? There's no planning a sneeze, is there? Was my thinking out of control?

Then I landed on a 2010 report by the BBC, on something that turned my thinking, about thinking, on its head. The neuroscientist, John-Dylan Haynes and his team at the Max Planck Institute in Germany, monitoring the activity patterns in specific areas of the brain, could predict which hand a participant would use, several seconds before the participant used that hand, to push a button, when prompted to do so. (Search: "Neuroscience and Free Will BBC video, Marcus Du Sautoy")

> "*Your decisions are strangely prepared by brain activity,*" Haynes clarified.

Ok — so *do I control that?!* Emotions were intensifying.

The implications of such research seemed to reveal that thinking, and therefore deciding/choosing, is happening before action is taken?! And, if hooked up to a monitor, others watching would know which hand I was going to use, before that hand acted — which astounded me, and many others!

I wondered if instead of watching brain regions on a monitor, could each of us naturally watch what's there on/in our brain/minds, as if there was a monitor there revealing thoughts, ideas, dreams . . . like a movie . . . Do we come equipped for that? Seems we do. So would watching our "inner-monitors" give us the richest, fullest life experience: reducing snapping-mad occurrences, while increasing peacefully balanced ones?

What about a true turnaround for those suffering from PTSD (Post-traumatic Stress Disorder)? Could "awareness training" be a remedy for soldiers, police, firefighters, etc.

who may suffer from their experience? Was that possible, by being trained to watch thoughts versus simply experience them?

Would I be in control of myself if I was aware, from patterning watching (observing), which associations came crashing-in shaking body, brain/mind and spirit into chaos; more-fully knowing what was happening? And w*ould observing those body-brain/mind combinations (emotions) naturally shift every outcome — profoundly?*

Can you tell me what you're going to think next, or what your body is going to do, next? Wait . . . I'm positive it'll come to you . . . yet that's far from being "in control" of what your next move and/or thought, or emotional response will be.

The field of brain research overflows with reports such as, *Brain Meet Gut*, in the October 2015 issue of the journal, *Nature*. The research pointed to "*a growing body of data,*" showing that, "*microbes in the gut influence behavior and can alter brain physiology and neurochemistry,*" (prompting mental and physical outcomes). We are now examining our "gut's" role in thinking and emotional expression! In the future will we acceptably say, *"My stomach made me do it!"?* Are we back to "information poisoning"?

All this points to the new understanding that our "brains" are not simply the mass of fat located in our heads. No joke. I also learned that fat is it's primary composition, approximately 60%! (National Library of Medicine, National Institutes of Health: https://www.ncbi.nlm.nih.gov/pubmed/20329590).

Then I came across information that reported that that fat in your head is connected at its base, (stem) to what scientists have named the "vagus nerve," *(it's all connected!),* and the microbes that live there spiral through the entire human body, which begs the question, "Well then, where the heck exactly is the brain/mind?" Do we need to enlarge our definition of "brain" to include more than just the fat? Did the content of the mind exist all over the place and not simply in the brain in our head?

Maybe we're essentially brain/minds-walking and, that entire body-brain/mind system is in process 24/7!, never turning-off until we're "dead." And, as a "brain/mind walking," decoding each of our sense abilities, each thought, idea, dream . . . which part of that, do "You", and "I," control?

Do we control the beating of our heart? Then how about the pulsing of our brain . . . mind? It mattered — *to an accurate sense of our identity.*

My original question stuck to me, although it was changing . . . *Was I actually wrestling with a language problem?* Was the word "control" simply language describing an experience *that doesn't actually happen, like "sunrise and sunset"?* We believe that! Yet, the Sun doesn't really "rise", nor does it "set." The Sun, as I understand it, is a burning star, a mass of plasmatic energy that does that moving-spiraling-ever-outward-thing, with the rest of the universe in formation . . . So, if the Earth is a moving, spinning, wobbling mass around the sun, and it's all spiraling in motion together — planets spinning around the sun, etc., and we continue to communicate "sunrise," or "sunset," we continue to tell inaccuracies, when we know better. And, we're all agreeing that it's ok . . . until we don't . . . Yet does anything change if you were to hear, or read on your local weather channel, *"Today in our area, the Earth will rotate toward the sun, at 7:07am, and rotate away from the sun at 7:10pm"?* How does that feel?

American writer, Samuel Langhorne Clemens, pen name, Mark Twain, wrote,
> *"It ain't what you don't know that gets you into trouble, it's what you know for sure that just ain't so."*

Is a legacy *understanding "that just ain't so,"* limiting us, compared to what we might experience regarding a new, accurate understanding of "control," *and human identity*, and our potential life experience?

Is suicide, homicide, accidents, and terroristic acts our system naturally processing information that it's absorbing from all around and then acting accordingly *and,* rather appropriately?

And, if you follow a thought back far enough, does it ever really end? And, if it does, did you choose that end? (Check out Prompt #11) . . . And, if we choose thoughts, are we choosing the best ones we can, the most advantageous? Why, or why not? Is our mind giving us good advice? Mine was on a roll!

Byron Katie, American author and facilitator, has a marvelous program called, The Work (thework.com). In it she asks one simple question, *"Who would you be without that thought?"* That question flings open the doors of the imagination (and awareness) . . . *"You mean I don't have to have that thought and those emotions?* Another thought and other emotions can happen?! Yes, they can. Revolutionary thinking?

"IT'S ALL YOUR FAULT!"

No one likes the sound of that coming from another, or from within. It's painful to be blamed, accused of, pointed to, for something that has caused *something "bad," pain.* It stirs potential sadness, shame, anger, and fear . . .

No one likes to be "blamed," thought of as "*bad*," (we want to know we are good!), and yet, *if we control our thoughts* as we learned, then "blame" is accurate and every one of us is responsible for what we think — 24/7.

I noticed that felt so heavy . . .

" . . . *the heart of any conversation is the demand being made on my emotions.*" Brilliantly said by, American writer, Hugh Prather.

Ironic "emotion" rhymes with "ocean," both so vast . . . associations were in the making . . .

For clarity, let's agree that "emotion" is defined as the togetherness of the body-brain/mind-spirit system. And that "togetherness" can be observed. So every thought is then connected to a physical response and every physical response is connected to a thought (idea, dream, etc.) — bar none — *and all of it, we can become aware of (observe).*

Considering that, would you say we plan on smiling, or does smiling just happen, like crying, or perhaps even thinking? I really considered all that . . . *do "I" plan my emotions . . . if I'm in control, or do they happen like sneezing?*

I am a trained *worrier*, not *warrior*. It became a pattern. My parents experienced World War II in their late teens, on the heels of the Great Depression and people in America were intensely afraid (like today?). I absorbed my family's and society's worry, fear, as I was in relationship to all of it, even as they, and many others, went forth to create a good life.

So staying steady when the shit-hit-the-fan, seemed a life lesson for me to master; specifically when fear reared it's very ugly head . . . And, let me tell you, I've had my fair share of intensely fearful experiences and thoughts; from watching people I love being taken away by "the authorities," to being a single parent of two very young sons; being "let go" from a rather large financial Institution after it was acquired by another in the early 2000's, to barely earning an income for years after the 2008 U.S. financial crash and, the suicide of a dear friend of my youngest son. And let's include the experience of my home of almost 20 years sold in a Sheriff's Sale, while in an active foreclosure case. Those intensely frightening experiences were emotionally uncomfortable and exceptionally unpredictable. They were also accompanied by a slew of uncomfortable, unpredictable physical ailments. I felt and sensed it all deeply. *I was it all — walking, breathing.* Every single fearful, tearful thought, I lived and felt — *and it felt way beyond my control; which I was supposed to have.*

So what if thoughts do just arise? Are we all blameless for emotions that express themselves thoughtfully, physically, heroically, suddenly . . . ?

"No blame? Is that possible? Does someone have to take the blame, be at fault, responsible, for whatever happened? Does someone *really* need to be blamed? Can we truly pin blame on a specific cause? Like a thought, how far back does blame go? And, if we're all in relationship, in one functioning universal system — socially, naturally — aren't we then *all to blame*? And the same would apply to *"getting credit,"* yes? Would we all *get credit* for something achieved?

> *"Not a single person responsible for the 2008 recession has gone to jail! And — that's part of the anger of a huge number of people. How do we get past that?!"* His anger was still fresh, even though more than 10 years had passed.

Understanding from a scientific perspective that with thought, sparks fly from natural electrical and chemical firings throughout our body-brain/mind-spirit system, emotion can then be one word to describe all that *energy-in-motion* surging, pinging, happening every — moment. We've named such currents with a spectrum of words like paranoid, nauseous, anxious, sweaty, afraid, numb, hurt, stressed, yet no matter the word, they all describe a body-brain/mind event, experience.

Psychologist Kelly McGonigal's, *"How to make stress your friend,"* 2013 TED Talk, with over 16 million views, urges us to, *"see stress as a positive,"* and that we need to think of it as a kind of body and mind communication that is usefully informing us. Ok, so if we become aware of, observe our "stress," (what the body and mind experiences, because we can), does that immediately shift stress to calm? Thinking, was back to that again.

The word "observation," appeared in a spectrum of material I was reading about physics. The littlest things seemed to matter *(pun happened)*. In their book, *Quantum Enigma*, Bruce Rosenblum and Fred Kutter, wrote on p.12,

> *"Though quantum theory works perfectly, it says something weird; an object is created somewhere by our observation of it . . . Quantum theory has atoms and molecules not existing someplace <u>until our observation creates them there.</u> According to Heisenberg [Werner Heisenberg], they are not "real," just "potentialities."* [My underline.]

So just imagine that our thoughts and emotions were objects (things, molecular structures?), yet very much alive, spirited objects, just like your hand, your pet, a tree. Now imagine that we've all been trained in "observing" such objects, trained to notice what's there, thoughts, emotions, ideas, clouds . . . *trained so that noticing what's there, being experienced, occurred more often and for longer durations of time,* (there's definitely a pattern here). Would that reduce, even eradicate, the intensity of pain, or a violent impulse — to snap? In other words, if we were taught to observe our thoughts, would that experience defuse possible violent actions that might potentially be expressed, no matter what the thought?! *And does observing happen like thinking?* Could I control observing, yet not thinking? *Did observing need to become a pattern, a good habit too!?*

I had yet to meet someone who said to me, that they were well aware they were about to snap violently and still, they snapped. For once there is an awareness of the body's response, and any thoughts and imaginings that are present, their trajectory changes and, remarkably beneficially, (she "almost" threw the plate). I also found, that when there is an awareness of responses, people experiencing them, feel safer . . . why was that?!

And why — when I'm clearly aware of an experience happening — does a question arise too, (such as, *"What else is possible?"* Are we hardwired for questioning? Does a question shift the trajectory of thought too? "I'm aware of what I'm thinking, and I'm aware of what I'm feeling . . . what else is possible to think and feel?!" Hmmm . . .

Albert Einstein expressed, *"The field is the sole governing agency of the particle."* Did he mean that all matter moved because of something else, say, an unknown "field"?! And that matter didn't move itself?! I wondered if he also might have meant that "observation" might be "the field," that beneficially "governs" our thoughts, ideas, sense abilities, best-decisions . . . (our thoughts being particle-like too)!

What if we each took notice of our laughter, our shyness, fear, and what prompts it? What if we noted daily, the dynamic interdependence (relationship) of everything around us? What if we really observed this whole thriving, alive system — would our life be fantastically freer? What if we learned this in elementary school, age appropriate of course, would we eliminate long-term unemployment, poverty, terroristic-acts . . .? The questions appeared . . .

I was imagining that the 2015 Disney movie, *Inside Out*, got it right. In the movie there was a team of emotions running the dashboard in Riley's head (the main character) . . . no central "I" in control . . . So who, or what, was "running" the Team (the fast ones; S1's or slow ones, S2's — both)!?

Neuroscientist and author Jill Bolte Taylor wrote, *"I whole-heartedly believe that 99,999 percent of the cells in my brain and body want me to be happy, healthy and successful."*

Ought we be shifting away from an identification with a "central-point-of-Me" in control, to an aware, "whole-system-Me" in action, processing?

We're now well versed in working with Prompts. You've observed relationships, no matter how subtle, after chapter 4, patterns after chapter 5, what's being sensed by your entire system after chapter 7, and your Jekyll/Hyde after chapter 8; all of their experiences overlapping . . .

With this Prompt the focus is on emotions — the body-brain/mind combo — also a 3-minute, or more if you like, practice . . .

PROMPT #5:
SCAN YOUR EMOTIONS: Further observe associations . . .

Scanning our bodies and brain/minds together — in relationship — offers a huge amount of information about what's present, what's happening, at the moment, radically balancing our systems.

Sitting or standing, pause, close your eyes, inhale deeply, exhale fully and comfortably, 3x's with eyes closed. Then, with eyes open or closed, quickly notice what your whole system is expressing. Is it tired, vibrant? What are the thoughts there? Are they fearful, sad, angry, joyful . . . ? Scan your physical response along with what's streaming through your brain/mind. Pay attention to the partnership. What thoughts, imaginings, accompany the physical expression?

Then look around at the environment surrounding you. Does it bring on an expression of contentment, laughter, nausea, resentment? Just watch (with wonder), at whatever is noticed. Imagine all of it is communicating.

This is a body-brain/mind scan and we can notice the energy (emotion) surging through our system; "fast and/or slow."

If nothing seems to show up, no worries. Remain relaxed. The more this is practiced, the more is noticed. You will get into a rhythm of observing.

What kinds of emotions are there, as you scan your body, brain/mind and environment? This is a, "getting to know YOU" practice.

Emotions had captured my imagination . . . What was that all about? I am taught by a young shaman, "Imagination" is a, "nation of images."

I definitely went in for a closer look . . .

Watch the contents of my mind. Don't let the contents lead.

10. IMAGINATION ILLUMINATED INFORMATION

Is every thought really a new idea — the new linking of information, forming a new association? Or is the imagination another kind of capability, very different from thinking? Why both words? Words were important and, thinking of this before, had happened — the "language problem" (. . . sunrise/sunset?). Why did it come to me just now, to review the definitions of more words? And again, were words and their meanings getting in the way of understanding that thinking *was* happening, that "I" was a whole body-brain/mind-spirit system and that whole system *was* "in control," (whether I understood that or not) and that, was good?!

Having established an ego through language, did we distort an already naturally existing, balanced identity?

A quick look-up on Google began with the word,
Imagination:
Noun
1.   the faculty or action of forming new ideas, or images or concepts of external objects not present to the senses.
     •   the ability of the mind to be creative or resourceful.

• the part of the mind that imagines things.

Then Wikipedia...

> "Imagination . . . ability to form images, ideas, and
> sensations in the mind without any immediate input
> of the senses (such as seeing or hearing) . . .
> Imagination is a cognitive process used in mental
> functioning and sometimes used in conjunction with
> psychological imagery."

Doesn't "forming images, concepts, external objects" sound
the same as thinking? And how do we divorce "sensations in
the mind" from, " . . . immediate input of the senses (such
as seeing, hearing . . .)"? Aren't we always seeing, hearing —
sensing?! How would we turn that off? How could "external
objects" not be present to the senses? How could sensing be
excluded in a definition related to the brain/mind? Don't we
require sensing in order to imagine, dream . . . think?! Aren't
they a partnership? And, aren't we each a whole functioning
system, within a larger system — all of it together — with
us simply naming things, classifying, in order to know, and
then communicate and navigate the whole of it?!

How far into the rabbit hole was I?

Who among us was taught, or knows that in our bones, we
are a part of a natural, self-caring system? That
consideration was still sinking into my psyche. I was
imagining the serious need for the re-education of
(understanding), who we are and how we work — yes, our
identity. That was a pattern I was noticing, and words
mattered. They expressed specific realities about identity.

Six years after the publication of Louis Stevenson's *Jekyll and
Hyde*, Sir Arthur Conan Doyle (in 1892) issued the first of
his imaginatively ingenious Sherlock Holmes stories. When
later interviewed, Doyle told of a Professor he encountered

while studying medicine at the University of Edinburg (1876-1881). The Professor, Dr. Joseph Bell, taught his students the importance of observation; of "... *using all of one's senses, paying attention to their responses, to obtain the most accurate patient evaluation and diagnosis.*" Doyle also told the reporter that being taught "to observe, to pay attention," inspired his creation of the Sherlock Holmes character. Like Louis Stevenson, was Doyle too, drawn to explore the potential of human behavior and its patterns, in order to have a more informed human experience? We thrive on information. Yet do we control it?

> Again, "*There is something about being aware of a thought (or anything), that profoundly changes . . . everything . . .*" rings loud in my head. (p.56)

I was back to observing that former pattern of thinking, the one I promised to return to back in Chapter 7 (Sense Ability), it went like this . . . (and imagine it as a specific reality) . . .

> "What if I don't remember!? What if I forget the stuff I've written down?! What if there's stuff I don't even know, that I should, know and remember, what about that stuff!? . . . Do you really want to think that — again?!"
> *(Quite imaginative – eh?)*

Now imagine that thinking-dialogue continued to unfold like this . . .

> "Do you really think you're doing the remembering?"

> "Yes! Of course I'm doing the remembering!? Who else is there to do the remembering?!"

> "Well what if "remembering" isn't a verb, isn't a who doing something, but rather a "what in process"? What then?"

"What are you talking about!?!"

Paying attention to new thoughts was happening . . (the wildest stuff shows up) . . .

What if we made up (imagined, then established) a word such as, *"remember"* to describe an experience we imagined — believed — we were having, because that's how that experience was first understood, and then taught, and passed on? It felt right at the time, and we didn't know any better. Essentially, you could say, we are making words up, and then passing the word-baton on to the next generation . . . And now, some of those meanings are inaccurate. It's how scientific-explorer-types have been advancing our understanding for hundreds of years!

> *You mean the sun is the center of an orbiting planetary sky-system, not earth?!*

That one must have thrown everyone completely off, for a 100 years!

So do we really control, "remembering," what is and isn't remembered? And where is that boundary . . . and *"Where are my damn keys?!"* and how come I can't remember?! I was told I was in control of my thinking!

That kind of thinking bothered me. It felt powerless. Which felt inaccurate.

. . . Another quick look-up on Google offered:
Remember:
Verb
1.   have in, or be able to bring to one's mind an awareness of (someone or something that one has seen, known, or experienced in the past).

And this from Merriam Webster . . .

> 2. to bring to mind or think of again
> 3. to keep in mind for attention or consideration

". . . *bring to one's mind* . . . "? How do I do that? I was imagining the word "remember" no longer described an accurate process — unless *"bring to one's mind"* was driven by a trigger, which was part of an entire system . . .

So what if there really is no "me" causing something (some sort of information) to return? What if information "returning" was simply a pattern happening in response to prompts, triggers? *"Remember"* Marcel Proust (. . . that was a prompt)? What if images, sounds, aromas, etc. "return" on their own, naturally, because of prompting by stimuli versus a, "who/ego," controlling something to, "return," and then that "who/ego" managing all those "returns/recollections"? Make sense?

And if I believe the word "memory" actually describes something accurate, I'd have to consider the storage of all that information, all those "memories" I absorbed over a lifetime. Which becomes a matter of location. Where is the information I want?

Then there is the retrieval of the information. Which has been considered for centuries. Once I go there, I'm back at having to "control" retrieval — the act of remembering, (and I don't think I can *do* that). And it doesn't seem to fit, now that we know so much more. I no longer believe the words "retrieval," or "remember" describe the process of information "returning" accurately.

Information seems to "return," arrive, with prompts, triggers, stimuli.

And, if we still feel we're in control of our thinking (all that "returning"), we would never be upset about not remembering a meeting, a birthday, to pick up coffee on the way home, because we'd remember everything, right? Our life would be perfect with us in control of our thinking, remembering and, our actions. Hmmm . . .

> *"Every so often some name, or thing, just pops into my head —*
> *having nothing to do with the time, place, or whatever's going on*
> *at the moment. It's an untethered thought, as if it got loose from*
> *where it was moored. Very curious . . . "*

Dad was describing thinking accurately.

Also from Google . . .
Control:
Noun

1. the power to influence or direct people's behavior or the course of events . . .

Noun

1. determine the behavior or supervise the running of
2. take into account (an *extraneous factor that might affect results*) when performing an experiment.

And the Merriam Webster Dictionary,
Control:
transitive verb

1. #2: to exercise restraining or directing influence over

Where in any of that, does it explain who, or what is driving the bus — "determining, directing, influencing" all that? Who the heck were these words giving agency to!?

So, maybe we're not in control of our thinking . . . at least not in the way we were taught. And what if no central-you (ego?) in control was better, or better yet, *no longer mattered?*

What if since birth, that entire body-brain/mind-spirit system had been *deciding, choosing and intending* as a whole system, to stay alive, without a, "You/me," individual, ego, central-point, in *control?*!

What if the system, in its infinite ways, in processing intensities of electric-alive impulses into inner and outer sensing, visioning, hearing, smelling, etc. (21+?), is patterns of information forming, emerging and, that authentic control is naturally in process, navigating us through life? . . . Versus "some-You-in-control," thinking it all up? What if "remembering" really is a set of patterns which show up in response to stimuli and, *we can learn to watch all that?* (repeating was definitely happening . . .)

And then there was *The New York Times, Science Times section* (Tuesday, May 28, 2019), reporting on Dr. Frances Arnold, receiving the Nobel Prize in Chemistry. It was one of her quotes that triggered my exhale . . . *"Give up the thought that you have control. You don't. The best you can do is adapt . . . sense the environment and respond."* (Master "Animal mind . . ." ?)

After a fair amount of time down this rabbit hole, I imagined much more about,

> *Do we think up everything we think . . . about, or does thinking JUST happen?*

I slowly understood that there is no, "central-point-of-you/me," him, her, that chooses, decides, determines, etc. what thoughts to think, or what to imagine. Thinking and imagining, dreaming, etc., is rather a whole body-brain/mind-spirit system in action, within a larger universal system in action, of which we can be aware, when trained. And to set that in motion requires a series of triggers too!

What if we embraced that knowledge about who we are and how we function? Would we know ourselves, positively differently?

Had researching and observing the question for so long, shifted my relationship to it, diminishing its intensity, charting a new understanding . . . simply by "paying attention to it"?!

Is this how authentic control works?

This catapulted me unexpectedly into . . .
1) becoming aware that patterning our ability to observe the thinking, and imagining that was happening at any moment, and then
2) noticing the physical responses happening in relationship with all that; our bodies to the rest of nature (and civilization),

proved crucial to a life well-lived; lessening the duration of pain and limitation. Providing balance sooner.

I was gob-smacked by such a reorientation!

> *"Watch the contents of my mind. Don't let the contents lead."*
> Hmmm . . .

Psychologist Dan Gilbert in his TED Talk, *Stumbling on Happiness*, mentions we all come equipped with a "pre-frontal cortex" (the front region of our brain), which he likens to an, "experience simulator." We're equipped with an *'experience simulator'*?!! He then goes on to explain, *"We humans can actually have experiences in our heads before we play them out here."* Yes, and we do, and that's owning some crazy-amazing equipment!

Who needs to buy virtual reality gear, when it's built-in to us! Just close your eyes and watch!

As Dr. Seuss proclaimed, *"Oh the thinks you can think!"*

Here's a fun Prompt to stimulate the observation of your imaginings . . . Read first, then do . . .

PROMPT #6:

SEA OF BELIEFS: Sometimes I call this practice, "cliff notes" . . .

Have pen and paper near, for this Prompt.

Sitting is best. When you're ready, pause, close your eyes, inhale deeply, exhale fully and comfortably, 3x's with eyes closed.

Keeping eyes comfortably closed, imagine you are outside on a clear, beautiful day. The sun is shining, the air is soft and you are sitting on the ground, in the grass, five feet from the edge of a cliff.

You can see out over the edge — yet it's so vast you can't see land on the other side, nor can you see the bottom below.

What you can see is a sea of cloud-like misty substance, and you see words floating within it, shaped into sentences that form beliefs.

You understand this is "The Sea of Beliefs," comprised of only *outstanding beliefs*. You move closer to the edge and take a deeper look.

You're excited to reach over with one hand and pull out one of the *outstanding beliefs*. So you stick your hand into the swirling, cloud-like misty-nature, and pull one out. You notice it, pause, and note how the experience of it feels so good.

You decide you will remember it, (or maybe you write it down, by quickly opening your eyes, writing, and then closing them again. You might also wait till the end of the practice to write down the beliefs).

You place that belief by your side and reach in again for another. You swirl your hand around until it finds a match. You pull it out and view that one. You are amazed by that *outstanding belief* too. You notice the body-brain/mind experience of it and make note of it (writing or remembering it), as this belief also feels extraordinary and wonderful.

You place the 2nd belief next to you, beside the first one, and for the 3rd time, you reach into the Sea of Beliefs, swirl your hand around and grab a final *outstanding belief*. You notice that one, pause again, and make an observation of your experience of it, (and you write that one down too).

While considering all 3 beliefs and how good they feel, you gather them up, stand up, and with a toss all three go flying out of your hand, toward the vast sea, back into the misty, cloudy, wordy substance, and you thank them for showing up, as they did.

Begin to slowly open your eyes and come back to your space. If you haven't already, you may make note of the three beliefs you pulled from the sea.

This too, is an eye-opener. One in which you come face to face with an infinite number of outstanding possibilities, probabilities — such vast potential to experience.

When doing this Prompt, you may also hold a concern in mind, before you close your eyes and begin. You my intel for the outstanding beliefs you pull out, to inform you about your concern. Playing with imagining the Sea of Beliefs often, your thinking will positively shift and a pattern of observation will be strengthened.

If our natural ability to observe, was patterned to become aware of all our imaginings — Jekyll to Hyde — it seemed any thought, idea, dream, etc., could then be experienced with exceptional balance. Thoughts and imaginings would be seen, known. And that, seemed to matter.

The attributes of thinking and awareness made us humans akin to a kind of super-hero-creative-being; beneficially and sustainably enhanced.

It was ok that thinking wasn't a verb.

I now needed to zero in on observation . . .

I found myself relaxing into "a paradigm crisis."

11 OBSERVATION —
WE ALL COME EQUIPPED

The Bible even states in Jeremiah 6:17, *"I set a watchman over you saying, hearken to the sound of the trumpet"*; that we require training, experiential education, to know what's there, (sound the Trumpet!). We can become aware of the intangible conceptual stuff and, we love it when we do, (we love knowing)! And, knowing our thoughts, ideas, dreams, environments, etc., radically changes life for the better. Evolution at its best?

Let's revisit that former pattern of thinking once again, to make another point about thinking, and our natural ability to observe . . .

Here's the former thought pattern,
> "What if I don't remember!? What if I forget the stuff I've written down?! What if there's stuff I don't even know, that I should, know and remember, what about that stuff!? . . .

Now notice a new, possible pattern:
> "I'm aware of the thoughts, *"What if I don't remember!? What if I forget the stuff I've written down?! etc., etc. . . . ?!"* Yet, I'm also aware of how my body feels in relationship to those thoughts. It's clear certain thoughts feel better than others.

With this new pattern of understanding, thinking is then experienced as a communication, an action informing us, (Kelly McGonigal's *"make stress your friend"?*). The new pattern may sound unusual, yet perhaps only because it's new, (*"The Earth will be rotating toward the sun at 7:07am . . . and rotating away . . .)*.

Though what a difference a new, more accurate, pattern makes.

And if, *"What if I forget! . . . ?",* is the only thought streaming through our entire system, then that is, and will be, our only reality until the thought changes, driven by some trigger. Make sense? Which may be a reason to pattern McGonigal's, *"How to make stress your friend,"* and understand "stress," as information we can become aware of and in so doing, we move into a balanced state. It seems only natural.

There is a big difference between,
> #1.
> *"I forgot," "I didn't remember, recall, or think of that."* (Lots of blame and fear there.)

and . . . the consolidated version,
> #2.
> *"Noticing that didn't happen."* Period.

How simple can we get?! What relief! No blame.

I found myself relaxing into "a paradigm crisis."

The brain is ever-reformatting itself and that's good. It means new ideas can be considered and take hold. Science has been reporting it's "plastic" for some time; able to know something new; form new patterns. We now accept and believe such research. Scientists in other fields seem to report the same — *that nature renews itself for the best possible outcome.* Amazing!

We can observe and know about much of what's here, even if we can't detect the infrared light waves seen by a snake, or hear frequencies dogs can, (without equipment we create). We've got quite a set of natural attributes that navigate what's here, and the attribute to "be aware of," just may be our species' crowning glory . . .

Has a good life for all of us always been a matter of what's running through our minds (and bodies) *and knowing if?* Has observation, for most of us, been unknown and therefore naturally dormant, till now?

There is clearly more for us to tap into, than just experiencing all that conceptual content of the brain/mind.

Has thinking, without any real awareness of it, held the reins of our experience far too long? Do we need to pivot our understanding, about what we now know, about how we work?

> *"To observe thinking, or not to observe thinking?"* was that really the question?!

Observing that quietly happened when another   question arrived . . .

> *"So what's the difference between being in 'the zone' like an athlete (experiencing any intense focus), and observing?"*

Answering questions seems to begin with associations!

Intense focus on something, is what I discovered regarding, "the zone." All thoughts and actions, including the environment are right for that specific experience. There is the flow of a very specific nature, everything happening highly synchronistically, for a specific outcome.

I wondered if it was accurate to say, that every day we are in "the zone" of our lives . . . Maybe it was time to snap out of it and into the observation of it . . .

The focus of observing was a kind of distance-big-picture-view of becoming aware of thoughts, ideas, dreams, the surrounding environment, the noticing of sound . . . a flow of sensing felt. There is no right, or wrong. There is no opinion, as any opinion would be sensed and observed too. There is no aimed-for outcome. Observation is an intimate, in-your-face knowing — with no real meaning about what's experienced. Just an experiencing. It's personal. Close, as if what's observing, is observing its enjoyment — knowing itself in a far greater way. Knowing seemed key to balance.

I bet you know both experiences; the zone and observing.

And, during those moments in which you were observing — so very aware of something — you may have even noticed something more . . .

Chögyam Trungpa, was raised to be a supreme (Buddhist) Abbot of the Surmang monasteries in Tibet. In his book, *Cutting Through Spiritual Materialism*, he so beautifully stated on page 222,

> " . . . *the color of the flower conveys a message over and beyond the simple perception of color. There is great meaning in this color, which is communicated in a powerful, almost overwhelming way. Conceptualized mind* [thoughts/ideas?] *is not involved in the perception and so we are able to see with great precision . . ."* [My words in brackets.]

Experiential evidence demonstrating that if you observe, with all of your sense ability, you may experience the energetic movement generating the color of the flower Chögyam Trungpa speaks of — for a truly, potentially unlimited, richer life.

"Do you want that?," emerged . . .

As we experience more of our human potential we might consider that the attribute of observation is the whole system's rudder, keeping the journey of life on track.

Imagine for a moment that you're sitting in the first row of an elegant theater. The house lights dim, the music comes up, along with the curtain and a spotlight. You see the most amazing scene slowly unfold. The actors are so close. You can see the spit flying as their emotions intensify, yours do too. The stage, scenery, lighting, wardrobe — *all of it* — make the play seem absolutely real. It's all so visceral. At that moment, you are immersed in the story with heightened senses, experiencing its moments. You are in it. Possibly, completely absorbed. For that moment, it is your reality. (The "zone"?)

Then, it's intermission. Houselights go up. You look around. People are moving about, and you get up and move from the front row of the theater, up to the balcony and take an empty seat. Intermission ends and the theater goes dark. You begin to watch the performance from there. You now see not only what's happening on stage, the orchestra in the pit, you see all the seats in the hall, the audience, ornate wallpaper and moulding, chandeliers, how high the ceiling is . . . whatever is in that theater space that's possible to see, you begin to notice — to observe all of it. Now you are watching the play, as well as, what it's in relationship to — in this case, the entire performance theater; the exit signs, Ushers, and so on. And, with such perspective, comes a different and fuller experience. You like the front row, yet the balcony brings a greater knowing (. . . and we love to know).

It's the same outside the performance hall, once back on the street. We require both experiences *for an optimal life*; the "*in it*" (zone?), and "*observing the, in it*"! Still with me?

Here's a current example of the Importance of knowing both:

By September 23, 2018, the news in the U.S. continued its reporting of a possible replacement of two Supreme Court Justices; Antonin Scalia, who had died in 2016, and Justice Anthony M. Kennedy, who had just announced his retirement.

Brett M. Kavanaugh, a judge on the U.S. Court of Appeals for the District of Columbia was nominated, and from the ether appeared Dr. Christine Blasey Ford, a woman who maintained that she had experienced attempted rape by Kavanaugh in high school, 36 years back. The focus of the story, "*Is this man suitable, or not suitable for the position* — on the highest court in the land — for life"*?*

That was the thinking — only — the "in it" focus and, it dominated the news. It was a front row perspective. And we all had front row seats (to the performance). We were in it; "Is this man . . . is this woman . . . " You could see the spit flying as emotions — theirs and ours — intensified.

Now imagine we all stay in our seats for the entire program, right there, *in the front row*, close up, and by the end, we find ourselves dramatically exhausted and frustrated, and seriously "in it." It is our reality, and there is no way out — no place to move to, and no one feels good in a "no way out" story. "This is me! That's you!" was all that existed.

Even the President had a front row — only — perspective.

Next is a screen shot taken on September 23, 2018, showing "front-row-seat thinking" . . .

Ford/Kavanaugh on Twitter
https://twitter.com/search/Ford%2FKavanaugh

Donald J. Trump (@realDonaldTrump)	ChuckGrassley (@ChuckGrassley)	Donald J. Trump (@realDonaldTrump)
I have no doubt that, if the attack on Dr. Ford was as bad as she says, charges would have been immediately filed with local Law Enforcement Authorities by either her or her loving parents. I ask that she bring those filings forward so that we can learn date, time, and place!	Judge Kavanaugh I just granted another extension to Dr Ford to decide if she wants to proceed w the statement she made last week to testify to the senate She shld decide so we can move on I want to hear her. I hope u understand. It's not my normal approach to b indecisive	The radical left lawyers want the FBI to get involved NOW. Why didn't someone call the FBI 36 years ago?
2 days ago · Twitter	1 day ago · Twitter	2 days ago · Twitter

→ View on Twitter

With the Kavanaugh/Ford story, most of those watching, had not yet walked up to the balcony to watch from a greater perspective and know that the issue was not only, *"Is this man suitable, or not . . . and why is this woman sharing her truth. . . "* yet rather what a balcony view might have provided is this question, "Why do some voters want a Supreme Court Justice who is conservative; or non-conservative; or one who can observe both extremes, to lead a just system and, what are the concerns and benefits of these positions — for everyone?"

When observing, we not only see the topic, the focal point, the object (the spit), we also see *more possibilities*. We see what's all around, (the spit and its relationships), and then question — what else is possible? Without a balcony view we are radically limited and choices are then made from limited-perspective patterns. Those result in confining outcomes.

For me, in it's own crazy way, observation is the focusing in on something in particular, in order to see its relationships — observing to see everything — the potential infinite number of probable, possible working parts, so best resolutions can take shape.

Observing begs us to, "go large," which seems also to be the space in which human innovation occurs, offering greater solutions, resolutions, best decisions . . . We are at our best when there is an A, B, C, and so on. We don't thrive in limitation. Does anything?

Which is why getting our attribute of observation in motion to happen for more people, more often, is now critical; so we don't remain only in the front row with a limited view . . . *"is this man, is this woman . . . ?"* That was the smaller aspect, of the larger concern.

In a nutshell, without observation (awareness) in process, we live the limited "story" as if it's the only reality possible; a kind of living bondage. Without awareness in play, we limit our life experience. And if one of us is limited, we are all limited.

Kavanaugh was only a symbol of what we wanted, or didn't want — a conservative, a non-conservative, a balanced observer, or otherwise — presiding on the bench. The Kavanaugh/Ford story caused many to realize, 1) what is it we really want and, 2) Who do we want to lead us there?

Regarding leadership, C. Otto Scharmer states in the Introduction to his book, Presence, (2004, co-authored by Peter Senge, Joseph Jaworski and Betty Sue Flowers),

> *This blind spot concerns not the what and how — not what leaders do and how they do it — but the who: who we are and the inner place or source from which we operate, both individually and collectively.*

Saturday, October 27, 2018, my cell phone reports: Gunman kills 11 at a Pittsburg Synagogue. The gunman, 46, had a pattern of hate. That's all he knew. Was that all he was trained to know? Is that how his kind of training expresses itself — in killing?

Who of us is being trained to hate, and why? Do we all take credit and blame?

Was hate and fear simply faith in evil? What about faith in good? Did good exist naturally and was evil man-made? Had I absorbed a lifetime of faith in evil!?

I thought this was incredible too . . .

> *"More perplexing is that these two contradictory behaviors of love and hate are seemingly polar opposites. How could these contradictory behaviors possibly be controlled by the same set of neurons in the hypothalamus?"* (an area of the brain) — *Why We Snap*, by R. Douglas Fields, Ph.D.

Where was their borderline?!

We were all trained in certain stories, cultures, religions, politics . . . and *that is,* who we think we are?

When we begin to observe that training, seeing the relationships of the meanings of those stories; when we move to the balcony and watch from there, we see way more information and the stories naturally recalibrate, providing greater understanding. We thrive on a big-picture view.

I now believe, 1) we possess two miraculous natural abilities — thinking (and let's include with that imagining, dreaming, sensing . . .), and 2) observation, the awareness of all of the above, and our environment.

These two attributes are surely our species' internal natural scales of justice, and when trained to know them, they provide exactly what we need and yearn for — balance.

And, being "in control" as we know it, is no longer required. We can now relieve our psyche of that, just by setting awareness practices in motion . . . And, no blame?! . . . Was that part of the payoff?

. . . no human is left out.

12. THE PAYOFF . . .

For a species that questions, loves to know, and loves to discover what's new, observing our thoughts, ideas, environments, bodies, etc. satisfies us fully.

And observing, is a matter of practice. We've practiced everything we know.

Without practicing, learning about the experience of both thinking and observing, we can be destructive and unintentionally unaware of it, missing the richness of a big-picture experience. Then we are unable to positively shape the most beneficial, and sustainable, private (individual), and social (group) systems.

Thinking and imagining, without observation of it, can send us to our death.

We require more than those abilities that may be currently engaged for a remarkable life. And, we *all* come equipped, with that something more.

> That an awareness of my thoughts (ideas, dreams, all that conceptual stuff) could happen, and in becoming aware of all that, after practice and patterning, a peacefully balanced feeling would happen too — was astounding to me. Was that like observing a potential

particle, right out of its potential wave, toward a more beneficial trajectory — one of natural good?

Once we are aware of something — anything — sensing it, is a kind of knowing it, and once something is known, we are in a new experience with it.

So, what do you think?

Is our ability to observe, the self-caring experience that balances the potential chaos of the body-brain/mind? Does our attribute of observation cancel out the the intensity of any potential Mr. Hyde?!

. . . And no human is left out.

If the awareness of our thoughts happened more often, seems the payoff was that we could . . .

- Stop berating and blaming ourselves, our kids, family, friends, co-workers, enemies, and so on, for not acting, behaving, doing, implementing, planning, not remembering, or being able "make up their mind", choose, or decide, "just stop it", "just be happy", "let go", or keep resolutions.

  What then when blame, (and let's add punishment too), are not required for a thriving society, or culture?

- Educate young and old, to engage their full potential, by which to experience life. To experience their minds uniquely, feel their ideas viscerally, know their body's sense abilities, in relation to all that's here.

- Understand ourselves as being in relationship to everything, and that all of it requires some other aspect of itself — of what's here — for its very existence. This could become everyday conviction, setting into motion emotional and ecological wellbeing; for humans and the rest of nature.

How fully do we want to experience our life?

- Put down the sword of control; the long-lived burden that we are "in control" of what we think and do, and instead, spend more time setting observation in motion through practice, which balances the process of thinking, imagining, dreaming, etc., offering an equalized, safe experience for all.

  What if thinking happened and, you could be aware of what's there, would control, as we now understand it, matter?

- Become more aware of our thoughts and that alone will naturally shift our *identity-understanding —* *who we think we are* — which is currently the single greatest factor in all human acts of violence; suicide to terrorism.

  What if the human attribute, "to be aware of" was understood as our "identity," our "Self," rather than the information we may accept without question, over a lifetime, from those, who tell us who we are? Would that shift anything?

- Understand the paramount importance of all information. We may begin to pause and ask, *"Is this information useful — good for me, us, the whole of what's here?*

We may become even more discerning about what we absorb and then create.

Since we have the potentiality of genius — imagining amazing things — we will begin to feel the need to manifest only those ideas which beneficially advance everything; *e.g., maybe we'd return to raking leaves, versus power-blowing them; eliminating air and noise pollution. Yes it would be more labor — yet the benefits are clear.*

- Understand that Innovative, decision-making and effortless-collaboration will naturally be set in motion.

Noticing the new, is the imaginative capacity locking into place, and we are hard-wired for that. It's inherent in wanting to know. And, we become much more satisfied and content, as more possibilities (information) associate and come into awareness.

Creating solid think-tanks and maker-spaces, redirecting what's uncomfortable, (or even dreadfully off-course), will happen individually and en masse. A win-win; reducing potential destructive and violent acts.

> NOTE: *I find that answers are finite and in their own fashion, can be limited. In relationship however, all answers stimulate more questioning, which is why innovation will pop from all of us, as we become more aware of the thinking, questioning and answers that are happening.*

- Understand that every age group will render violent unpredictable thinking, a non-issue as, no human will fear another. They will instead, become aware of their fearful thoughts, rendering them balanced.

Unpredictability will remain — yet absent of human violence. (I'd risk setting observation in motion for that!)

- Finally put fear, victimhood and powerlessness to rest; yours, mine, their's . . .

When thinking just happens and observation is our pattern . . .

- We may — globally — celebrate, explore, and experience our powerfully creative, *common attributes*: observing, thinking, imagining, intuiting, dreaming. . . with excitement; for perhaps the first time in a very long time.

Life may feel like it's falling into a natural rhythm, flow, grace and ease — for all.

Can you feel that the "pay-off" is fantastically great news?!

You are not your mind." was Sir John Hargrave's call, in his book, Mind Hacking. And then I came upon this, by the late physicist, David Joseph Bohm, *"a former colleague of Albert Einstein at Princeton, whom Einstein regarded as an intellectual successor,"* (noted in, Presence, p.189),

> *"Thought runs you. Thought, however, gives the false info that you are running it, that you are the one who controls thought. Whereas actually thought is the one which controls each of us . . . Thought is creating divisions out of itself and then saying that they are there naturally . . . thought doesn't know it is doing something and then it struggles against what it is doing . . . I call this 'sustained incoherence.'"*

I was standing on the shoulders of giants . . .

Yes, let's become more aware of all that thinking (imagining, sensing, emoting), happening and capitalize on setting that in motion — our inherent ability to observe. Let's invent more products, curricula, events, websites, media sources, movies, fashion, food, toys, therapies, and so on, that flood the market establishing such a possible, sustainable at-peace balance — for all.

Now that you've absorbed the information here, any new associations happen? Are you becoming more aware of your thoughts?

Does thinking happen as a whole body-brain/mind-spirit-nature, etc. system? I think so. I think that's a more accurate understanding. And it's uncanny how accuracy always feels better . . .

Can we be aware enough to observe that system happening, for best actions to occur, for a brilliant life to happen, for the potential elimination of suicide, homicide, accidents, and the unlawful use of the environment that sustains us? I think so — when taught. We come equipped for that.

What are we thinking? It matters.

And if I've completely snapped, I welcome anyone, including those at higher education and/or research institutions, as well as lone-wolf researchers, to contact me at, info@danalichtstrahl.com and show me why. *As I can hardly believe all this myself.*

*To be aware of a thought, and its potential,
is to set our fullest potential, for good, in motion.*

13. CONTINUING TO SET OBSERVATION IN MOTION . . .

" . . . *I am exhausted. The scene I have imagined is
detailed, brutal and unbearable. I cannot live through what I
anticipate. I stop. I refuse to experience that imaginary
assault again.*" – Toni Morrison

Celebrated American novelist, Toni Morrison, so beautifully
expresses an experience of the body-brain/mind-spirit, in
the above quote. It is physically painful, unwelcome and
unpredictable. Yet, she is aware of the thought, and its
potential, full-blown, experience emerging. "*I stop.*" She
writes, "*I refuse to experience that imaginary assault again.*" And
just maybe, that's the moment the psyche and body are
beneficially balancing; recalibrating, self-correcting; *aware of*
its thinking.

Our systems inform us electrically, linguistically, sensually,
and on and on . . . of what's there. And we can know.

Continuing to work with the Prompts in this chapter will set
observation in motion more frequently . . .

Along with practicing the Prompts, I also began prompting
myself with yellow sticky notes . . . With a bold black
marker I wrote the same word in all caps, on several notes:

WATCH. I put them everywhere. In the bathroom, on the refrigerator, on my computer monitor, my car's rear view mirror, everywhere I'd notice it. The word was meant to prompt me to pause and observe my physical and mental responses, to become present — externally, internally — of all I could, (according to 21+ senses). The repetition of seeing "WATCH," worked to strengthen a pattern of pausing and observing. So paying attention, happened more often, even when no note was present. It was a pattern-strengthening workout. The days became richer and more balanced because of it. I'm excited by this awareness-pattern continuing to show up. I'm much more of an observation-warrior now, then a worrier.

Truly consider that "You" don't need to "be in control." I know, that may still feel like an upside down idea. Let's just say, "You" (all of us; our systems) just require more useful patterning. And new prompts over time, such as the ones that follow, will establish "more useful" patterns.

Considering you came equipped with the hardware and software to notice thoughts, ideas, beliefs, dreams — all that intangible stuff that arrives on your sense-radar, "playing attention," (yes, playing with attention) to the practices here, is the goal. Play and have fun.

To be aware of a thought and its potential, is to set our fullest potential, for good, in motion.

As author and spiritual leader Alan Cohen, so perfectly stated in one of his very first books, *The Dragon Doesn't Live Here Anymore*, *"If you always do, what you've always done, you'll always get, what you've always gotten."* (Wow. repetition counts.)

And to that I say, next time you sit down to watch a movie, or get up to wash the dishes, make that call, or walk the dog, instead, "play attention" for 3-minutes, to any one of the Prompts in this book. 3-minutes is a long time. Then watch the movie., walk the dog, etc.; which may turn out to be an entirely richer experience.

> 1) a. Read through the prompt, b. try it out, c. notice (reflect on) the experience of the prompt.

> 2) Try the prompts often. Yet whether 3 or 33-minutes of engagement, once, or multiple times a day, you will be beneficially changed in some way.

> Can't say enough about that. Imagine the water contained within your body — something like 60%. Now imagine how water shifts from the slightest stimuli, a leaf, a breeze, practicing . . . get the association?

. . . And, while experiencing all that and the prompts, just suppose our fantastic attributes — thinking and observing — makes us humans, a guardian and steward of all that's here . . . the watchers (observers) over all life; yours, mine, his, hers, that mountain, forest, fox, flower, honey bee — while all that life supports our very existence in return . . .

I think that's truly great news. What do you think?

. . .

*. . . the root of heaven and earth.
It goes on and on, something which almost exists;
Use it, it never runs out.
— Book of the Yellow Emperor*

MORE EXCITING PROMPTS TO EXPERIENCE AND PLAY ATTENTION TO . . .

PROMPT #7
WHAT ARE YOU FEELING? IT MATTERS:
Scan your body . . . **A, B**

A: Next time you're outside walking down the street, take notice of how your body feels. What kinds of responses are happening when walking by a row of houses, a block of businesses, a park, an empty car lot, etc.? Stay alert to your system's expression. This is such an insightful experience, patterning observation. If your mind offers varied thoughts, notice those too. How is all of you responding?

B: If you're eating, focus on noticing how the food feels in your mouth; texture, temperature, and so on. Go slow. Notice how wide you have to open your mouth to take in food, or drink . . . Have you ever "played attention" to what you put in your mouth? Now is the time.

When noticing, when *really* playing attention to what's being sensed — experienced — you activate more of your potential, and life becomes beneficially bigger and maybe even feels more grounded and rock-solid.

Having a greater experience here *continues to happen* as you practice noticing your body's responses to triggers, etc. You get to know you; what your body likes and what it doesn't, and maybe even why. You get to know your unique sensations. *You really get to deeply know your system — maybe for the very first time.*

So . . . what's being sensed right now? Daily, take a moment and observe and hear the question within. . . Best habits don't get any better than the habit of knowing what you're sensing. Set that in motion!

PROMPT #8:

WHAT DO YOU THINK? IT MATTERS TOO:
Scan your mind, watch your opinions . . . **A, B**

A: Scanning our minds can be more elusive than scanning the body. The stuff of the mind seems so untouchable, unknowable, intangible. How do we get our arms around that? Yet, thoughts, ideas, dreams can also be sensed as very solid — like a Rock-solid opinion.

We live what's on our minds each day. It's our front row seat. *We are so close to it, we think it is us, our identity;* the truest story we know, until we know something new. For many, it's not easy to observe a thought. It can be like trying to see the tip of your nose.

So first imagine an apple. Any apple. Notice its color, shape, what's around it. What do you think, about that apple? Does it feel good or not so good, to see it? If you had an opinion about the apple, what might it be?

Now shift your focus to noticing "opinions" about things in your immediate space. Do you like the furniture in the room, how about the art on the walls. Look around. What's your opinion? What is your whole system experiencing — picking-up? What opinions, arise when you observe what's there? Do you hear them? See, smell them? Or are opinions more like movie clips you get to watch?

Let's take this further. If I ask you your opinion of a movie, a restaurant, or about something in the news, a response will show up, like some sort of object flying onto your radar. That's noticeable too. Observe how your body feels in relation to opinions.

Observing your opinions can happen anytime, anywhere. Just watch . . . play attention to them . . .
B: Now *scan your brain/mind to observe* any thoughts about the past, or future. Is there a thought about something you must do now? Somewhere you must go, or how you did in this morning's meeting? Maybe something that occurred when you were young, and it's arriving now. Just notice what's there.

Again, consider each thought like you would an object like a laptop, a lamp, a coin . . . Do this enough, and pausing randomly to brain/mind-scan (knowing what's there) will naturally happen and pattern — for your benefit.

Q & A: *So why is knowing what's arriving and fading in your brain/mind important?*

Knowing thoughts diminishes their experienced intensity; balancing the experience. It also offers new possibilities, due to questions that follow the awareness of a thought. Which offers a very different life-experience then simply experiencing a thought, (through the emotional-spectrum of possible associations). So, *see it to see through it* and learn that you are not what's in/on your brain/mind; more accurately, you are what's aware of it. And we all share that in common.

Scanning and observing what's happening, breaks that *interwoven "in it"* experience, and offers you the whole quilt, versus a few threads. You may realize a sense of freedom, liberation and an overall, more balanced sense of you. Practicing, patterning is the mastery. Like memorizing an alphabet, numbers, days of the week, and walking.

Take a moment and thoroughly, slowly scan your brain/mind . . . What's being noticed right now?

PROMPT #9:
DISTANCE LISTEN: To everything . . .

This is quick. Take 1 minute and 30 seconds, sitting, standing, or walking, (not while driving), and listen for what you can hear. That's it. Just listen.

What can you hear that's furthest away? Notice that thoroughly. Listen to the distant barking dog, church bell, people talking way over there, car horns in traffic several blocks away, a siren, the wind . . .

Just listen for distant sounds, vibrations. Turn up the dial on those antenna-ears and notice what's heard. If you begin to notice close-up sounds, something next to you, that's ok. Notice those sounds in relationship to the distant sounds. Then focus again on the distant ones, those that are truly far away. Any new ones show up that weren't initially noticed?

Feel your way into hearing what's there.

Do you like what's heard, yes, no? Why? What is your whole body-brain/mind-system receiving — *for your ears (whole system) only?*

For this prompt, you are simply practicing becoming much more aware of what's heard by your unique ears — and all the senses they are connected to which make hearing so visceral, possible, sensual. While listening, also keep in mind, that without the sun, air, water, earth, . . . your ears would be very different. And that, is miraculous. You may even begin to feel a reverence for the ability to hear/ listen. That right there, offers a richer life.

PROMPT #10:

SPECIFICALLY LISTEN TO YOURSELF SPEAK:
Anytime!: *A, B, C, D*

What do you sound like? Ever notice listening to yourself?

A: When the time is right, throughout a day, listen to you . . . speak. Because you can. Play attention to what you're saying to the cashier at the store, your colleagues at work, your friends, teachers, parents, etc. Listen in on every conversation you have. Do you like the words coming out of your mouth? Do you plan them? Can you plan them every time you speak, yes/no?

Few of us pay attention to what we say. Sounds so funny. Focus primarily on you and your mouth, those words, sounds, tone, timbre . . .

Whether in conversation by phone, video, face to face, etc. become aware of your inflection, maybe even the shape of your mouth when the words emerge . . . or where your tongue is, or what the rest of your body is doing in relationship. What's your forehead doing while you speak? Is it relaxed, wrinkled?

Do you like what you hear? If not, why not? If yes, why? Are certain words spoken, a pattern? Keep playing attention to hearing yourself speak.

B: We did this as kids: talk out loud when playing, busy with life, until maybe, someone told us to stop. Talking out loud is the surest way to learn and observe what's being thought, imagined, or stressed over.

So try this when the time and space you're in is comfortable, and just *talk out loud*. What do you hear?

What's the meaning there? Is it useful? . . . Did you know all of that was there, before you spoke and then listened?

C: Now let's take this one step further. *Listen past the words;* your's or another's, to only the sound. Kind of like listening to a foreign language; when there's no meaning in the words (because you don't know them) and yet, we might listen to the sound the words are making for the fun of it, to harvest that experience sensing it, or to know more about life.

Is there intensity, softness, high pitch, low grumbles . . . Is the *sound* of the words communicating, enhancing something, in relation the meanings of the words?
How about the pauses and silences, do they establish the sounds and meaning too?

Are we really translating frequencies into meaning and emotion — daily — and we've created, and use, many words to describe the vast frequency-experience?

When you can distinguish the words from their sounds, you are becoming a steller observer.

D: Ever hear your voice recorded or on video? What do you think about the sound of it? If you haven't and have a recording or video device, use it. Record what's on your mind during the day, and listen to it later. Listening to what comes out of your mouth, from an electronic device, offers further insight while patterning observation to happen often.

Getting to know what you sound like is a key experience of observation. [A shorter version of this prompt was posted on p.104 of "Are You Watching?" Amazon.com.]

PROMPT #11:

TRAIN OF THOUGHT: This can be quite fun, short and simple . . .

Have pen and paper handy for this Prompt in case you'd like to write, sketch, or diagram what you notice . . .

Sitting is best for this practice. When you're ready, pause, close your eyes, inhale deeply, exhale fully and comfortably 3x's, with eyes closed.

While keeping eyes comfortably closed, notice a thought, any thought will do. You can practice this anytime, anywhere, with any kind of thought. An especially intense thought will offer a different outcome than a more neutrally-felt thought, so try them one at a time . . .
Once you have noticed one, visualize, imagine, that *you are riding on that thought, like you can ride on a train,* going from one place to another. Now imagine that you are riding that "train of thought" to the very last station stop. Watch where it goes. Watch what goes by (other thoughts, scenes, imaginings?) As you ride that train of thought, does it change tracks, switch to another thought or image?

Sometimes I'm riding a train of thought and I'm off it way before I want to be.

Switching tracks of thought happens! What's your experience? The awareness attribute gets set in motion quickly with this practice too.

PROMPT #12:

PAST CREATIVITY: Let's play with the past.

You may want to have pen and paper handy for this Prompt too . . . This practice aims to stimulate imagination and in doing so, you get to observe creativity in action (it's very cool).

Sitting or standing, pause, close your eyes, inhale deeply, exhale fully and comfortably, 3x's with eyes closed. Really track the air being brought into your system and leaving it, yes, playing attention to what's happening, inside and out of body and brain/mind.

Then, slowly open your eyes and see if you notice an event from your past. Just one. The first one that shows up. Notice it, and maybe notice your age at that time, the environment, what and who was around . . .

Since you know what occurred after that moment in time, now is the time to imagine at least three new possible outcomes, that could have happened, from that same moment in time.

Viscerally feel, sense each possibility that might have unfolded. Go wild with imagining possible new outcomes! Bar none. See what shows up.

After you have imagined and focused on three (3) possibilities, imagine three (3) more? What else can you sense that might have happened after one-experienced past event?

Ok, now choose a different past event, and do the same practice, imagining new, possible events that *might* have happened from it, versus what did.

If you experience this practice deeply, sense-ually, you may experience your past very differently. Which may just beneficially shift your present . . . and future?

PROMPT #13:
NO NAMES: No thing has a name. Practice that!

Sitting or standing, pause, close your eyes, inhale deeply, exhale fully and comfortably, 3x's with eyes closed.
Take as much time with this one as you like. Your focus and patterns will be challenged.

For the next few minutes, imagine that there aren't any names for anything, not even you. Begin there. Just look around without knowing the name of anything, or rather pretending that you don't know the names of anything; the "chair" to your favorite "food." If you notice naming occurring, just observe the naming that's happening, and continue to look around and experience what's there, *without knowing any names* . . .

What remains of a thing when it has no name — including you?
Kind of curious, yes?

PROMPT #14:

JUST PAUSE AND TAKE 5: A 3-minute (or less) observational moment, anywhere, anytime, with or without anyone.

Pause . . . look around . . . at everything . . . What's noticed; rock to idea? Anywhere, anytime . . . That's it. Get into *that* practice, the rhythm of "pausing," taking a moment to look around and sense what's there.

Also look for where one thing ends and another begins, and look at the space in between. Is there any?

Do this daily and you will sense balance . . .

PROMPT #15:

USE THE OPPOSITE HAND: Just try this for one day — Ok, maybe an hour . . .

Use your non-dominant hand (the one you use less), for most of what you do: brush your teeth with your non-dominant hand, drink your coffee, write, draw, open doors, grab your cell phone, etc. You get the idea.

Shift what is currently your non-dominant hand, to the dominant position — even for one short hour, and notice if anything changes about your perception and perspective. Repeat often and observation will become second nature.

PROMPT #16:

YOUR PROMPT. New Prompts show up. We come equipped for that to happen. No one is left out . . . So if you happen to notice a new Prompt that you enjoy and sense it's particularly effective at setting, "the awareness of" in motion, educate us. Share it. Post your Prompt on social media.

There can never be too many Prompts to set observation in motion. If you'd like, email them to me at, info@danalichtstrahl.com and I'll post them on danalichtstrahl.com, with or without your name/link, as you like . . .

• • •

Can you imagine awareness prompts going viral?!

• • •

Your life is changing favorably — and because of that, everyone and everything is positively evolving (me included). Thank you.

Let's all keep playing attention to all the attributes we came equipped with. *It matters* . . .

What Are We Thinking? It Matters.

Outside of a dog, a book is a man's best friend;
and inside of a dog, it's too dark to read.
– Groucho Marx, American Comedian, 1890-1977

ACKNOWLEDGEMENTS; ABOUT

A deeply grateful, "Thank you!" to the best editor a writer could ever have, my dad, Dr. Melvin A. Benarde. He read and re-read, making significant edits and became an exceptional observer along the way. And to my brother, Scott Benarde, thank you too, for dotting all those "i"s and crossing all those "t"s early on, while imagining all those possible book titles — on your day off! To my mom, Anita Benarde, your questions and recommendations made the book a more powerful read. To my sister, Andrea Spiritos, thank you for your enthusiasm. It made a difference. It truly takes a village. Superior Project Manager, Sharon Rogers, your recognition of how important this project was to me, drove me to its completion and I sincerely thank you for that. I can't thank psychotherapist, Roberta Pughe, enough, for wanting my voice to be heard, and making suggestions so that might happen. A deeply heart-felt thank you to you, Dr. P., your crazy-kindness provided me time to play attention and write. And, a huge energetic burst of love to my sons, Zach and Jacob, for always supporting my diverse imaginings.

An autodidact by nature, I have multiple passions in both the arts and sciences. Most of all, I am fascinated by information, the process of thinking and observing, and

111

how all three affect and effect, who we think we are — and therefore how we behave, and what we create.

Human life is nothing short of miraculous, since we come with extraordinary attributes. My interest in this was sharpened by attending lectures at the Institute for Advanced Study and Princeton University, both in Princeton, NJ, and completing course work at the the Scared Trust, in the U.K. I hold a BA from University of Maryland, in studio art and communication, having also studied fine art at the Instituto de Allende in GTO, Mexico.

I now facilitate the fun learning of our potential — our remarkable abilities to think and observe — so we may become aware of the internal dialogue, for a better external experience; a win-win for all.

I'm an in-depth fan of anthropology, theatrical and visual arts, biology, cosmology, dance, drumming, dogs, music, nature, philosophies, physics, psychologies, and spiritual wisdom traditions, which I weave into my work. (Well maybe not the dogs.)

Communication has been my sandbox for over 30 years. Early on I was a news graphic artist at WJZTV in Baltimore, when Oprah Winfrey was there as a local news reporter and talk show host . . . *You can't make this stuff up!*

Later, for a major financial institution, I oversaw communication, marketing, events, and charitable giving.

My books, which focus on identity, can be purchased on Amazon: *A Case of Mistaken Identity, a not-so-fable FABLE* (fiction); *Are You Watching? (non-fiction); Jackson's Love (fiction romance);* and *not-so-fable Fables (a fiction collection).*

And, GOOSE the app is coming! GOOSE will startle, prod, prompt, and urge you toward great moments of new associations, insight and awareness . . .

Here's a GOOSE to prompt you now;

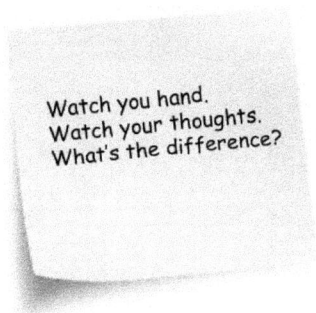

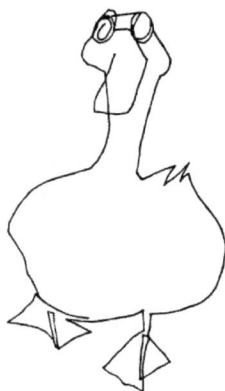

Watch you hand.
Watch your thoughts.
What's the difference?

Copyright 2019 Dana Lichtstrahl

Stay in touch . . .
info@danalichtstrahl.com; danalichtstrahl.com

www.ingramcontent.com/pod-product-compliance
Lightning Source LLC
Chambersburg PA
CBHW060527030426
42337CB00015B/2002